JavaScript®
Essentials

by Paul McFedries

A Wiley Brand

JavaScript® Essentials For Dummies®

Published by: **John Wiley & Sons, Inc.**, 111 River Street, Hoboken, NJ 07030-5774, www.wiley.com

Copyright © 2024 by John Wiley & Sons, Inc., Hoboken, New Jersey

Published simultaneously in Canada

For general information on our other products and services, please contact our Customer Care Department within the U.S. at 877-762-2974, outside the U.S. at 317-572-3993, or fax 317-572-4002. For technical support, please visit https://hub.wiley.com/community/support/dummies.

Wiley publishes in a variety of print and electronic formats and by print-on-demand. Some material included with standard print versions of this book may not be included in e-books or in print-on-demand. If this book refers to media such as a CD or DVD that is not included in the version you purchased, you may download this material at http://booksupport.wiley.com. For more information about Wiley products, visit www.wiley.com.

Library of Congress Control Number: 2024933533

ISBN 978-1-394-26321-9 (pbk); ISBN 978-1-394-26323-3 (ebk); ISBN 978-1-394-26322-6 (ebk)

SKY10072504_041224

Contents at a Glance

Table of Contents

Introduction

HTML and CSS are awesome technologies, and you can use them to create pages that look amazing. But after you funnel your page to your web server and look at it a few (dozen) times, you may notice a subtle feeling of disappointment creeping in. Why? It can be hard to pin down, but that hint of dismay comes from a stark fact: Your web page just kind of sits there.

Sure, you probably have a link or three to click, but most likely those links just take you to more of your pages that also just kind of sit there. Or maybe a link takes you to another site altogether, one that feels dynamic and alive and interactive. Ah, engagement! Ooh, excitement!

What's the difference between a page that does nothing and a page that seems to be always dancing? One word: JavaScript. If you want your pages to be dynamic and interactive, you need a bit of behind-the-scenes JavaScript to make it so.

"But," I hear you object, "HTML isn't that hard to learn. JavaScript is a programming language, for crying out loud!" I hear you. It's true that anyone can learn HTML as long as they start with the basic tags, examine lots of examples of how they work, and slowly work their way up to more complex pages. It's just a matter of creating a solid foundation and then building on it.

I'm convinced that JavaScript can be approached in much the same way. I'm certainly not going to tell you that JavaScript is as easy to learn as HTML. That would be a bald-faced lie. However, I will tell you that there is nothing inherently difficult about JavaScript. I believe that if you begin with the basic syntax and rules, study tons of examples to learn how they work, and then slowly build up to more complex scripts, you can learn JavaScript programming. I predict here and now that by the time you finish this book, you'll even be a little bit amazed at yourself and at what you can do.

About This Book

Welcome, then, to *JavaScript Essentials For Dummies*. This book gives you a solid education on the standard programming language underlying the World Wide Web. You learn how to set up the tools you need and, given any web pages you have (or someone else has) built with HTML and CSS, you learn how to use JavaScript to program those pages. My goal is to show you that adding a sprinkling of JavaScript magic to a page isn't hard to learn, and that even the greenest rookie programmer can learn how to create dynamic and interactive web pages that will amaze their family and friends (and themselves).

If you're looking for lots of programming history, computer science theory, and long-winded explanations of concepts, I'm sorry, but you won't find it here. My philosophy throughout this book comes from Linus Torvalds, the creator of the Linux operating system: "Talk is cheap. Show me the code." I explain what needs to be explained and then I move on without further ado (or, most of the time, without any ado at all) to examples and scripts that do more to illuminate a concept that any verbose explanations I could muster (and believe me, I can muster verbosity with the best of them).

Foolish Assumptions

This book is not a primer on the internet or on using the World Wide Web. This is a book on coding web pages, pure and simple. This means I assume the following:

>> You know how to operate a basic text editor, and how to get around the operating system and file system on your computer.

>> You have an internet connection.

>> You know how to use your web browser.

>> You know the basics of HTML and CSS.

Yep, that's it.

Icons Used in This Book

REMEMBER

This icon points out juicy tidbits that are likely to be repeatedly useful to you — so please don't forget them.

TIP

Think of these icons as the fodder of advice columns. They offer (hopefully) wise advice or a bit more information about a topic under discussion.

WARNING

Look out! In this book, you see this icon when I'm trying to help you avoid mistakes that can cost you time, money, or embarrassment.

Where to Go From Here

How you approach this book depends on your current level of coding and/or JavaScript expertise (or lack thereof):

>> If you've never programmed before, begin at the beginning with Chapter 1 and work at your own pace sequentially through Chapters 2, 3, 4, and 5. This will give you all the knowledge you need to pick and choose what you want to learn throughout the rest of the book.

>> If you've done some non-JavaScript programming, start with Chapter 1, skim through Chapters 2 through 5 to see how JavaScript does the standard programming tasks, and then pick and choose your topics from there.

>> If you've done some JavaScript coding already, I suggest working quickly through the material in Chapters 2 through 5, and then diving into the all-important material on the Document Object Model in Chapter 6. From there, you can peruse the rest of the chapters as you see fit.

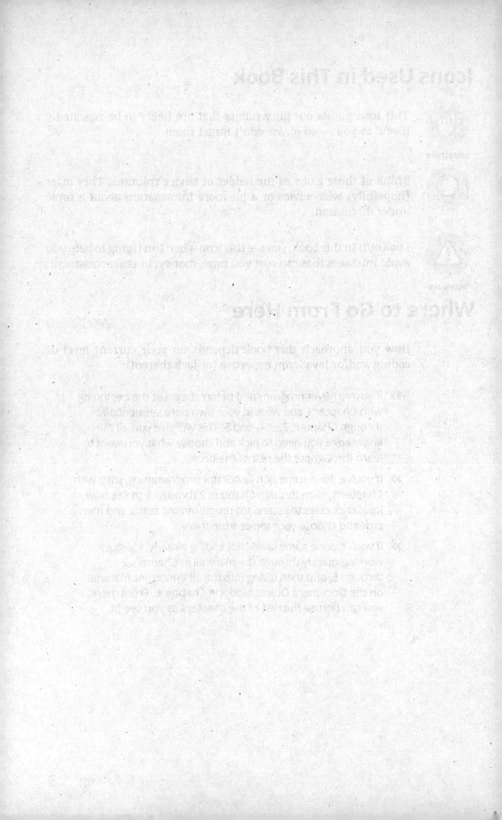

IN THIS CHAPTER

» Getting a feel for programming in
general, and JavaScript in particular

» Checking out the tools you need
to get coding

» Adding comments to your
JavaScript code

» Storing your code in a separate
JavaScript file

Chapter 1

JavaScript: The Big Picture

I n this chapter, you explore some useful JavaScript basics. Don't
worry if you've never programmed before. I take you through
everything you need to know, step-by-step, nice and easy. As
you're about to find out, it really is fun to program.

Adding JavaScript Code to a Web Page

Okay, it's time to roll up your sleeves, crack your knuckles, and
start coding. This section describes the standard procedure for
constructing and testing a script and takes you through a couple
of examples.

The <script> tag

The basic container for a script is, naturally enough, the HTML
<script> tag and its associated </script> end tag:

```
<script>
    JavaScript statements go here
</script>
```

Where do you put the <script> tag?

With certain exceptions, it doesn't matter a great deal where you put your <script> tag. Some people place the tag between the page's </head> and <body> tags. The HTML standard recommends placing the <script> tag within the page header (that is, between <head> and </head>), so that's the style I use in this book:

```
<!DOCTYPE html>
<html lang="en">
    <head>
        <meta charset="utf-8">
        <title>Where do you put the script tag?
</title>
        <script>
            JavaScript statements go here
        </script>
    </head>
    <body>
    </body>
</html>
```

Here are the exceptions to the put-your-script-anywhere technique:

>> If your script is designed to write data to the page, the <script> tag must be positioned within the page body (that is, between the <body> and </body> tags) in the exact position where you want the text to appear.

>> If your script refers to an item on the page (such as a form object), the script must be placed *after* that item.

>> With many HTML tags, you can add one or more JavaScript statements as attributes directly within the tag.

REMEMBER

It's perfectly acceptable to insert multiple <script> tags within a single page, as long as each one has a corresponding </script> end tag, and as long as you don't put one <script> block within another one.

Example #1: Displaying a message to the user

You're now ready to construct and try out your first script. This example shows you the simplest of all JavaScript actions: displaying a basic message to the user. The following code shows the script within an HTML file:

```
<!DOCTYPE html>
<html lang="en">
    <head>
        <meta charset="utf-8">
        <title>Displaying a Message to the User
</title>
        <script>
            alert("Hello JavaScript World!");
        </script>
    </head>
    <body>
    </body>
</html>
```

As shown in here, place the script within the header of a page, save the file, and then open the HTML file within your browser.

This script consists of just a single line:

```
alert("Hello JavaScript World!");
```

This is called a *statement,* and each statement is designed to perform a single JavaScript task. Your scripts will range from simple programs with just a few statements to huge projects consisting of hundreds of statements.

You may be wondering about the semicolon (;) that appears at the end of the statement. Good eye. You use the semicolon to mark the end of each of your JavaScript statements.

In the example, the statement runs the JavaScript `alert()` method, which displays to the user whatever message is enclosed within the parentheses (which could be a welcome message, an announcement of new features on your site, an advertisement for a promotion, and so on). Figure 1-1 shows the message that appears when you open the file.

FIGURE 1-1: This "alert" message appears when you open the HTML file containing the example script.

How did the browser know to run the JavaScript statement? When a browser processes (*parses*, in the vernacular) a page, it basically starts at the beginning of the HTML file and works its way down, one line at a time. If it trips over a `<script>` tag, it knows one or more JavaScript statements are coming, and it automatically executes those statements, in order, as soon as it reads them. The exception is when JavaScript statements are enclosed within a *function*, which I explain in Chapter 5.

WARNING

One of the cardinal rules of JavaScript programming is "one statement, one line." That is, each statement must appear on only a single line, and there should be no more than one statement on each line. I said "should" in the second part of the previous sentence because it is possible to put multiple statements on a single line, as long as you separate each statement with a semi-colon (;). There are rare times when it's necessary to have two or more statements on one line, but you should avoid it for the bulk of your programming because multiple-statement lines are diffi-cult to read and to troubleshoot.

Example #2: Writing text to the page

One of JavaScript's most powerful features is the capability to write text and even HTML tags and CSS rules to the web page on-the-fly. That is, the text (or whatever) gets inserted into the page when a web browser loads the page. What good is that? For one thing, it's ideal for time-sensitive data. For example, you may want to display the date and time that a web page was last modified so that visitors know how old (or new) the page is. Here's some code that shows just such a script:

```
<!DOCTYPE html>
<html lang="en">
    <head>
        <meta charset="utf-8">
        <title>Writing Data to the Page</title>
    </head>
    <body>
        This is a regular line of text.<br>
        <script>
            document.write("Last modified: " +
    document.lastModified)
        </script>
        <br>This is another line of regular text.
    </body>
</html>
```

Notice how the script appears within the body of the HTML document, which is necessary whenever you want to write data to the page. Figure 1-2 shows the result.

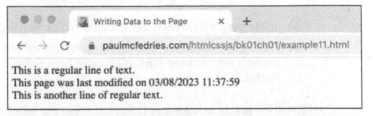

FIGURE 1-2: When you open the file, the text displays the date and time the file was last modified.

This script makes use of the document *object*, which is a built-in JavaScript construct that refers to whatever HTML file (document) the script resides in (check out Chapter 6 for more about the document object). The document.write() statement tells the browser to insert whatever is within the parentheses to the web page. The `document.lastModified` portion returns the date and time the file was last changed and saved.

What You Need to Get Started

One of the nicest things about HTML and CSS is that the hurdles you have to leap to get started are not only short but few in number. In fact, you really need only two things, both of which are free: a text editor to enter the text, tags, and properties; and a browser to view the results. (You'll also need a web server to host the finished pages, but the server isn't necessary when you're creating the pages.) Yes, there are high-end text editors and fancy graphics programs, but these fall into the "Bells and Whistles" category; you can create perfectly respectable web pages without them.

The basic requirements for JavaScript programming are exactly the same as for HTML: a text editor and a browser. Again, programs are available to help you write and test your scripts, but you don't need them.

Dealing with Two Exceptional Cases

In this book, I make a couple of JavaScript assumptions related to the people who'll be visiting the pages you post to the web:

>> Those people have JavaScript enabled in their web browser.

>> Those people are using a relatively up-to-date version of a modern web browser, such as Chrome, Edge, Safari, or Firefox.

These are pretty safe assumptions, but it pays to be a bit paranoid and wonder how you may handle the teensy percentage of people who don't pass one or both tests.

Handling browsers with JavaScript turned off

You don't have to worry about web browsers not being able to handle JavaScript, because all modern browsers have supported JavaScript for a very long time. You may, however, want to worry about people who don't support JavaScript. Although rare, some folks have turned off their browser's JavaScript functionality. Why would someone do such a thing? Many people disable JavaScript because they're concerned about security, they don't want cookies written to their hard drives, and so on.

To handle these iconoclasts, place the `<noscript>` tag within the body of the page:

```
<noscript>
   <p>
      Hey, your browser has JavaScript turned
   off!
   </p>
   <p>
      Okay, cool, perhaps you'll prefer this <a
   href="no-js.html">non-JavaScript version</a> of
   the page.
   </p>
</noscript>
```

If the browser has JavaScript enabled, the browser doesn't display any of the text within the `<noscript>` tag. However, if JavaScript is disabled, the browser displays the text and tags within the `<noscript>` tag to the user.

To test your site with JavaScript turned off, here are the techniques to use in some popular browsers:

- **Chrome (desktop):** Open Settings, click Privacy and Security, click Site Settings, click JavaScript, and then select the Don't Allow Sites to Use JavaScript option.

- **Chrome (Android):** Open Settings, tap Site Settings, tap JavaScript, and then tap the JavaScript switch to off.

- **Edge:** Open Settings, click the Settings menu, click Cookies and Site Permissions, click JavaScript, and then click the Allowed switch to off.

- **Safari (macOS):** Open Settings, click the Advanced tab, select the Show Develop Menu in Menu Bar, and then close Settings. Choose Develop ⇨ Disable JavaScript.

>> **Safari (iOS or iPadOS):** Open Settings, tap Safari, tap Advanced, and then tap the JavaScript switch to off.

>> **Firefox (desktop):** In the Address bar, type **about:config** and press Enter or Return. If Firefox displays a warning page, click Accept the Risk and Continue to display the Advanced Preferences page. In the Search Preference Name box, type **javascript**. In the search results, look for the `javascript.enabled` preference. On the far right of that preference, click the Toggle button to turn the value of the preference from `true` to `false`.

Handling very old browsers

In this book, you learn the version of JavaScript called ECMAScript 2015, also known as ECMAScript 6, or just ES6. Why this version, in particular, and not any of the later versions? Two reasons:

>> ES6 has excellent browser support, with more than 98 percent of all current browsers supporting the features released in ES 6. Later versions of JavaScript have less support.

>> ES6 has everything you need to add all kinds of useful and fun dynamic features to your pages. Unless you're a professional programmer, the features released in subsequent versions of JavaScript are way beyond what you need.

Okay, so what about that couple of percent of browsers that don't support ES6?

First, know that the number of browsers that choke on ES6 features is getting smaller every day. Sure, it's 2 percent now (about 1.7 percent, actually), but it will be 1 percent in six months, a 0.5 percent in a year, and so on until the numbers just get too small to measure.

Second, the percentage of browsers that don't support ES6 varies by region (it's higher in many countries in Africa, for example) and by environment. Most of the people running browsers that don't fully support ES6 are using Internet Explorer 11, and most of those people are in situations in which they can't upgrade (some corporate environments, for example).

If luck has it that your web pages draw an inordinate share of these older browsers, you may need to eschew the awesomeness of ES6 in favor of the tried-and-true features of ECMAScript 5. To that end, as I introduce each new JavaScript feature, I point out those that arrived with ES6 and let you know if there's a simple fallback or workaround (known as a *polyfill* in the JavaScript trade) if you prefer to use ES5.

Commenting Your Code

A script that consists of just a few lines is usually easy to read and understand. However, your scripts won't stay that simple for long, and these longer and more complex creations will be correspondingly more difficult to read. (This difficulty will be particularly acute if you're looking at the code a few weeks or months after you first coded it.) To help you decipher your code, it's good programming practice to make liberal use of comments throughout the script. A *comment* is text that describes or explains a statement or group of statements. Comments are ignored by the browser, so you can add as many as you deem necessary.

For short, single-line comments, use the double-slash (//). Put the // at the beginning of the line, and then type your comment after it. Here's an example:

```
// Display the date and time the page was last
   modified
document.write("This page was last modified on " +
   document.lastModified);
```

You can also use // comments for two or three lines of text, as long as you start each line with //. If you have a comment that stretches beyond that, however, you're better off using multiple-line comments that begin with the /* characters and end with the */ characters. Here's an example:

```
/*
This script demonstrates JavaScript's ability
to write text to the web page by using the
```

```
document.write() method to display the date and
    time the web page file was last modified.

This script is Copyright Paul McFedries.
*/
```

WARNING

Although it's fine to add quite a few comments when you're just starting out, you don't have to add a comment to everything. If a statement is trivial or its purpose is glaringly obvious, forget the comment and move on.

Moving to External JavaScript Files

Earlier in this chapter, I talk about adding JavaScript code to a web page by inserting the ⟨script⟩ and ⟨/script⟩ tags into the page header (that is, between the ⟨head⟩ and ⟨/head⟩ tags), or sometimes into the page body (that is, between the ⟨body⟩ and ⟨/body⟩ tags). You then write your code between the ⟨script⟩ and ⟨/script⟩ tags.

Putting a script inside the page in this way isn't a problem if the script is relatively short. However, if your script (or scripts) take up dozens or hundreds of lines, your HTML code can look cluttered. Another problem you may run into is needing to use the same code on multiple pages. Sure, you can just copy the code into each page that requires it, but if you make changes down the road, you need to update every page that uses the code.

The solution to both problems is to move the code out of the HTML file and into an external JavaScript file. Moving the code reduces the JavaScript presence in the HTML file to a single line (as you'll learn shortly) and means that you can update the code by editing only the external file.

Here are some things to note about using an external JavaScript file:

>> The file must use a plain text format.

>> Use the .js extension when you name the file.

>> Don't use the `<script>` tag within the file. Just enter your statements exactly as you would within an HTML file.

>> The rules for when the browser executes statements within an external file are identical to those used for statements within an HTML file. That is, statements outside of functions are executed automatically when the browser comes across your file reference, and statements within a function aren't executed until the function is called. (Not sure what a "function" is? You get the full scoop in Chapter 5.)

To let the browser know that an external JavaScript file exists, add the `src` attribute to the `<script>` tag. For example, if the external file is named `myscripts.js`, your `<script>` tag is set up as follows:

```
<script src="myscripts.js">
```

This example assumes that the `myscripts.js` file is in the same directory as the HTML file. If the file resides in a different directory, adjust the `src` value accordingly. For example, if the `myscripts.js` file is in a subdirectory named `scripts`, you use this:

```
<script src="scripts/myscripts.js">
```

You can even specify a file from another site (presumably your own!) by specifying a full URL as the `src` value:

```
<script src="http://www.host.com/myscripts.js">
```

As an example, the following code shows a one-line external JavaScript file named `footer.js`:

```
document.write("This page is Copyright "
    + new Date().getFullYear());
```

This statement writes the text "Copyright" followed by the current year. (I know: This code looks like some real gobbledygook right now. Don't sweat it, because you'll learn exactly what's going on here when I discuss the JavaScript Date object in Chapter 8.)

The following code shows an HTML file that includes a reference for the external JavaScript file:

```html
<!DOCTYPE html>
<html lang="en">
    <head>
        <meta charset="utf-8">
        <title>Using an External JS File</title>
    </head>
    <body>
        <p>
            Regular page doodads go here.
        </p>
        <hr>
        <footer>
            <script src="footer.js">
            </script>
        </footer>
    </body>
</html>
```

When you load the page, the browser runs through the HTML line by line. When it gets to the `<footer>` tag, it notices the external JavaScript file that's referenced by the `<script>` tag. The browser loads that file and then runs the code within the file, which writes the Copyright message to the page, as shown in Figure 1-3.

FIGURE 1-3: This page uses an external JavaScript file to display a footer message.

IN THIS CHAPTER

» **Understanding variables**

» **Assigning names to variables**

» **Introducing JavaScript data types**

» **Figuring out numbers**

» **Stringing strings together**

Chapter **2**

Programming with Variables

By default, JavaScript programs live a life without short-term memory. The web browser executes your code one statement at a time until there are no more statements left to process. It all happens in the perpetual present. Ah, but notice that I refer to this lack of short-term memory as the "default" state of your scripts. It's not the only state, so that means things can be different. You have the power to give your scripts the gift of short-term memory, and you do that by using handy little chunks of code called variables. In this chapter, you delve into variables, which is a fundamental and crucial programming topic. You investigate what variables are, what you can do with them, and how to wield them in your JavaScript code.

Getting Your Head around Variables

Why would a script need short-term memory? Because one of the most common concepts that crops up when coding is the need to store a temporary value for use later on. In most cases, you want to use that value a bit later in the same script. However, you may also need to use it in some other script, to populate an HTML form, or as part of a larger or more complex calculation.

For example, your page may have a button that toggles the page text between a larger font size and the regular font size, so you need some way to "remember" that choice. Similarly, if your script performs calculations, you may need to set aside one or more calculated values to use later. For example, if you're constructing a shopping cart script, you may need to calculate taxes on the order. To do that, you must first calculate the total value of the order, store that value, and then later take a percentage of it to work out the tax.

In programming, the way you save a value for later use is by storing it in a variable. A *variable* is a small area of computer memory that's set aside for holding a chunk of program data. The good news is that the specifics of how the data is stored and retrieved from memory happen well behind the scenes, so it isn't something you ever have to worry about. As a coder, working with variables involves just three things:

>> Creating (or *declaring*) variables

>> Assigning values to those variables

>> Including the variables in other statements in your code

The next three sections fill in the details.

Declaring a variable with let

The process of creating a variable is called *declaring* in programming terms. All declaring really means is that you're supplying the variable with a name and telling the browser to set aside a bit of room in memory to hold whatever value you end up storing in the variable. To declare a variable in JavaScript, you use the let keyword, followed by a space, the name of the variable, and the usual line-ending semicolon. For example, to declare a variable named interestRate, you use the following statement:

```
let interestRate;
```

REMEMBER

Here are a few things to bear in mind when you're declaring variables in your scripts:

>> **Declare a variable only once:** Although you're free to use a variable as many times as you need to within a script, you declare the variable only once. Trying to declare a variable more than once will cause an error.

>> **Use a comment to describe each variable:** Variables tend to proliferate to the point where it often becomes hard to remember what each variable represents. You can make the purpose of each variable clear by adding a comment right after the variable declaration, like so:

```
let interestRate; // Annual interest rate for
    loan calculation
```

>> **Declare each variable before you use it:** If you use a variable before you declare it, you'll get an error.

REMEMBER

In the first two items here, when I say that you'll "get an error," I don't mean that an error message will pop up on the screen. The only thing you'll notice is that your script doesn't run. To read the error message, you need to access your browser's web development tools, a task I go into in satisfying detail in Chapter 9.

>> **Declare each variable right before you first use it:** You'll make your programming and debugging (refer to Chapter 9) life much easier if you follow this one simple rule: Declare each variable just before (or as close as possible to) the first use of the variable.

REMEMBER

The let keyword was introduced in ECMAScript 2015 (ES6). If you need to support really old browsers — I'm looking at you, Internet Explorer 11 and earlier — then use the var keyword instead.

Storing a value in a variable

After your variable is declared, your next task is to give it a value. You use the assignment operator — the equals (=) sign — to store a value in a variable, as in this general statement:

```
variableName = value;
```

Here's an example that assigns the value 0.06 to a variable named interestRate:

```
interestRate = 0.06;
```

Note, too, that if you know the initial value of the variable in advance, you can combine the declaration and initial assignment into a single statement, like this:

```
let interestRate = 0.06;
```

It's important to remember that, given a variable declared with the `let` keyword, you're free to change that variable's value any time you want. For example, if the value you assign to the `interestRate` variable is an annual rate, later on your code may need to work with a monthly rate, which is the annual rate divided by 12. Rather than calculate that by hand, just put it in your code using the division operator (/):

```
interestRate = 0.06 / 12;
```

As a final note about using a variable assignment, take a look at a variation that often causes some confusion among new programmers. Specifically, you can set up a statement that assigns a new value to a variable by changing its existing value. Here's an example:

```
interestRate = interestRate / 12;
```

If you've never come across this kind of statement before, it probably looks a bit illogical. How can something equal itself divided by 12? The secret to understanding such a statement is to remember that the browser always evaluates the right side of the statement — that is, the expression to the right of the equals sign (=) — first. In other words, it takes the current value of `interestRate`, which is 0.06, and divides it by 12. The resulting value is what's stored in `interestRate` when all is said and done. For a more in-depth discussion of operators and expressions, head over to Chapter 3.

REMEMBER

Because of this evaluate-the-expression-and-*then*-store-the-result behavior, JavaScript assignment statements shouldn't be read as "variable *equals* expression." Instead, it makes more sense to think of them as "variable *is set to* expression" or "variable *assumes the value given by* expression." Reading assignment statements this way helps to reinforce the important concept that the expression result is being stored in the variable.

Checking out another way to declare a variable: const

The word *variable* implies that the value assigned to a variable is allowed to *vary*, which is the case for most variables you declare. Most, but not all. Sometimes your scripts will need to use a value that remains constant. For example, suppose you're building a calculator that converts miles to kilometers. The conversion factor is 1.60934, and that value will remain constant throughout your script.

It's good programming practice to store such values in a variable for easier reading. However, if you use let for this declaration, you run the risk of accidentally changing the value somewhere in your code because variables declared with let can change.

To avoid accidentally changing a value that you want to remain constant, you can declare the variable using the const keyword instead. Here's the general syntax:

```
const variableName = value;
```

Note that, unlike with let, you must assign a value to the variable when you declare it with const. Here's an example that declares a variable named milesToKilometers and assigns it the value 1.60934:

```
const milesToKilometers = 1.60934;
```

REMEMBER

Are there any real advantages to using const over let in cases where a variable's value must never change? Yep, there are two pretty good ones:

>> Using the const keyword is a reminder that you're dealing with a nonchanging value, which helps you to remember not to assign the variable a new value.

>> If you do try to change the value of a variable declared with const, you'll generate an error, which is another way to remind you that the variable's value is not to be messed with.

Given these advantages, many JavaScript programmers declare every variable with const and use let only for the variables that they know will change. As your code progresses, if you find that a const variable needs to change, you can go back and change const to let.

Using variables in statements

With your variable declared and assigned a value, you can then use that variable in other statements. When the browser comes across the variable, it goes to the computer's memory, retrieves the current value of the variable, and then substitutes that value into the statement. The following code presents an example:

```
let interestRate = 0.06;
interestRate = interestRate / 12;
document.write(interestRate);
```

This code declares a variable named interestRate with the value 0.06; it then divides that value by 12 and stores the result in the variable. The document.write() statement then displays the current value of the variable, as shown in Figure 2-1.

```
←  →  C    🔒 paulmcfedries.com/htmlcssjs/bk04ch02/example01.html

0.005
```

FIGURE 2-1: The browser substituting the current value of a variable.

The following code shows a slightly different example:

```
let firstName;
firstName = prompt("Please tell me your first
  name:");
document.write("Welcome to my website, " +
  firstName);
```

This script uses the prompt() method (explained shortly) to ask the user to enter their first name, as shown in Figure 2-2. When the user clicks OK, their name is stored in the firstName variable.

The script then uses a `document.write()` statement to display a personalized welcome message using the value of the `firstName` variable, as shown in Figure 2-3.

FIGURE 2-2: The script first prompts for the user's first name.

Welcome to my website, Alphonse

FIGURE 2-3: The script then uses the name to display a personalized welcome message.

When you need to get data from the user, run the `prompt()` method:

```
prompt(string, default);
```

Here's what the various parts are:

>> *string*: A string that instructs the user what to enter into the prompt box.

>> *default*: An optional string that specifies the initial value that appears in the prompt box.

The `prompt()` method always returns a value:

>> If the user clicks OK, `prompt()` returns the value entered into the prompt text box.

>> If the user clicks Cancel, `prompt()` returns `null`.

Naming Variables: Rules and Best Practices

If you want to write clear, easy-to-follow, and easy-to-debug scripts (and who doesn't?), you can go a long way toward that goal by giving careful thought to the names you use for your variables. This section helps by running through the rules you need to follow and by giving you some tips and guidelines for creating good variable names.

Rules for naming variables

JavaScript has only a few rules for variable names:

>> The first character must be a letter or an underscore (_). You can't use a number as the first character.

>> The rest of the variable name can include any letter, any number, or the underscore. You can't use any other characters, including spaces, symbols, and punctuation marks.

>> As with the rest of JavaScript, variable names are case sensitive. That is, a variable named InterestRate is treated as an entirely different variable than one named interestRate.

>> There's no limit to the length of the variable name.

>> You can't use one of JavaScript's *reserved words* as a variable name (such as let, const, var, alert, or prompt). All programming languages have a supply of words that are used internally by the language and that can't be used for variable names, because doing so would cause confusion (or worse).

Ideas for good variable names

The process of declaring a variable doesn't take much thought, but that doesn't mean you should just type in any old variable name that comes to mind. Take a few extra seconds to come up with a good name by following these guidelines:

>> **Make your names descriptive.** Sure, using names that are just a few characters long makes them easier to type, but I guarantee you that you won't remember what the variables represent when you look at the script down the road. For example, if you want a variable to represent an account number, use accountNumber or accountNum instead of, say, acnm or accnum.

>> **Mostly avoid single-letter names.** Although it's best to avoid single-letter variable names, such short names are accepted in some places, such as when constructing loops, as described in Chapter 4.

>> **Use multiple words with no spaces.** The best way to create a descriptive variable name is to use multiple words. However, because JavaScript doesn't take kindly to spaces in names, you need some way of separating the words to keep the name readable. The two standard conventions for using multi-word variable names are *camelCase*, where you cram the words together and capitalize all but the first word (for example, lastName), or to separate each word with an underscore (for example, last_name). I prefer the former style, so I use it throughout this book.

>> **Use separate naming conventions.** Use one naming convention for JavaScript variables and a different one for HTML identifiers and CSS classes. For example, if you use camelCase for multiword JavaScript variables, use dashes to separate words for id values and class names.

>> **Differentiate your variable names from JavaScript keywords.** Try to make your variable names look as different from JavaScript's keywords and other built-in terms (such as alert) as possible. Differentiating variable names helps avoid the confusion that can arise when you look at a term and you can't remember if it's a variable or a JavaScript word.

>> **Don't make your names too long.** Although short, cryptic variable names are to be shunned in favor of longer, descriptive names, that doesn't mean you should be using entire sentences. Extremely long names are inefficient because they take so long to type, and they're dangerous because the longer the name, the more likely you are to make a typo. Names of 2 to 4 words and 8 to 20 characters should be all you need.

Understanding Literal Data Types

In programming, a variable's *data type* specifies what kind of data is stored within the variable. The data type is a crucial idea because it determines not only how two or more variables are combined (for example, mathematically), but also whether they can be combined at all. *Literals* are a special class of data type, and they cover those values that are fixed (even if only temporarily). For example, consider the following variable assignment statement:

```
let todaysQuestion = "What color is your
    parachute?";
```

Here, the text "What color is your parachute?" is a literal string value. JavaScript supports three kinds of literal data types: numeric, string, and Boolean. The next three sections discuss each type.

Working with numeric literals

Unlike many other programming languages, JavaScript treats all numbers the same, so you don't have to do anything special when working with the two basic numeric literals, which are integers and floating-point numbers:

>> **Integers:** These are numbers that don't have a fractional or decimal part. So, you represent an integer using a sequence of one or more digits, as in these examples:

```
0
42
2001
-20
```

>> **Floating-point numbers:** These are numbers that do have a fractional or decimal part. Therefore, you represent a floating-point number by first writing the integer part, followed by a decimal point, followed by the fractional or decimal part, as in these examples:

```
0.07

3.14159

-16.6666667

7.6543e+21

1.234567E-89
```

Exponential notation

The last two floating-point examples require a bit more explanation. These two use *exponential notation*, which is an efficient way to represent really large or really small floating-point numbers. Exponential notation uses an e (or E) followed by the *exponent*, which is a number preceded by a plus sign (+) or a minus sign (-).

You multiply the first part of the number (that is, the part before the e or E) by 10 to the power of the exponent. Here's an example:

```
9.87654e+5;
```

The exponent is 5, and 10 to the power of 5 is 100,000. So, multiplying 9.87654 by 100,000 results in the value 987,654.

Here's another example:

```
3.4567e-4;
```

The exponent is -4, and 10 to the power of -4 is 0.0001. So, multiplying 3.4567 by 0.0001 results in the value .00034567.

Hexadecimal integer values

You'll likely deal with the usual decimal (base-10) number system throughout most of your JavaScript career. However, just in case you have cause to work with hexadecimal (base-16) numbers, this section shows you how JavaScript deals with them.

The hexadecimal number system uses the digits 0 through 9 and the letters *A* through *F* (or *a* through *f*), where these letters represent the decimal numbers 10 through 15. So, what in the decimal system would be 16 is actually 10 in hexadecimal. To specify a hexadecimal number in JavaScript, begin the number with a 0x (or 0X), as shown in the following examples:

```
0x23;
0xff;
0X10ce;
```

Working with string literals

A *string literal* is a sequence of one or more letters, numbers, or punctuation marks, enclosed either in double quotation marks (") or single quotation marks ('). Here are some examples:

```
"JavaScript Essentials";
'August 23, 1959';
"";
"What's the good word?";
```

REMEMBER

The string "" (or '' — two consecutive single quotation marks) is called the *null string*. It represents a string that doesn't contain any characters.

Using quotation marks within strings

The final example in the previous section shows that it's okay to insert one or more instances of one of the quotation marks (such as ') inside a string that's enclosed by the other quotation mark (such as "). Being able to nest quotation marks comes in handy when you need to embed one string inside another, which is very common (particularly when using bits of JavaScript within HTML tags). Here's an example:

```
onsubmit="processForm('testing')";
```

However, it's illegal to insert in a string one or more instances of the same quotation mark that encloses the string, as in this example:

```
"This is "illegal" in JavaScript.";
```

Understanding escape sequences

What if you must include, say, a double quotation mark within a string that's enclosed by double quotation marks? Having to nest the same type of quotation mark is rare, but it is possible if you precede the double quotation mark with a backslash (\), like this:

```
"The double quotation mark (\") encloses this
    string.";
```

The \" combination is called an *escape sequence*. You can combine the backslash with a number of other characters to form other escape sequences, and each one enables the browser to represent a character that, by itself, would be illegal or not representable otherwise. Table 2-1 lists the most commonly used escape sequences.

TABLE 2-1 Common JavaScript Escape Sequences

Escape Sequence	Character It Represents
\'	Single quotation mark
\"	Double quotation mark
\b	Backspace
\f	Form feed
\n	New line
\r	Carriage return
\t	Tab
\\	Backslash

The following code shows an example script that uses the \n escape sequence to display text on multiple lines with an alert box.

```
alert("This is line 1.\nSo what. This is line 2.");
```

Figure 2-4 shows the result.

FIGURE 2-4: Using the \n escape sequence enables you to format text so that it displays on different lines.

To learn how to combine two or more string literals, check out Chapter 3. Also, JavaScript has a nice collection of string manipulation features, which I discuss in Chapter 8.

Working with Boolean literals

Booleans are the simplest of all the literal data types because they can assume only one of two values: true or false. That simplicity may make it seem as though Booleans aren't particularly useful, but the capability to test whether a particular variable or condition is true or false is invaluable in JavaScript programming.

You can assign Boolean literals directly to a variable, like this:

```
taskCompleted = true;
```

Alternatively, you can work with Boolean values implicitly using expressions:

```
currentMonth === "August"
```

The comparison expression currentMonth === "August" asks the following: Does the value of the currentMonth variable equal the string "August"? If it does, the expression evaluates to the Boolean value true; if it doesn't, the expression evaluates to false. I discuss much more about comparison expressions in Chapter 3.

IN THIS CHAPTER

» Understanding what expressions are

» Figuring out numeric expressions

» Tying up string expressions

» Getting the hang of comparison expressions

» Learning about logical expressions

Chapter **3**

Building Expressions

When coding in JavaScript, you use expressions constantly, so it's vital to understand what they are and to get comfortable with the types of expressions that are available to you. Every JavaScript coder is different, but I can say without fear of contradiction that every *good* JavaScript coder is fluent in expressions.

This chapter takes you through everything you need to know about expressions. You discover some expression basics and then explore a number of techniques for building powerful expressions using numbers, strings, and Boolean values.

Understanding How Expressions Are Structured

A JavaScript *expression* takes one or more inputs, such as a bill total and a tip percentage, and combines them in some way — for example, by using multiplication. In expression lingo, the inputs are called *operands*, and they're combined by using special symbols called *operators*.

>> **operand:** An input value for an expression. It is, in other words, the raw data that the expression manipulates to produce its result. It could be a number, a string, a variable, a function result (refer to Chapter 5), or an object property (refer to Chapter 6).

>> **operator:** A symbol that represents a particular action performed on one or more operands. For example, the $*$ operator represents multiplication, and the + operator represents addition. I discuss the various JavaScript operators throughout this chapter.

For example, here's an expression that calculates a tip amount and assigns the result to a variable:

```
tipAmount = billTotal * tipPercentage;
```

The expression is everything to the right of the equals sign (=). Here, billTotal and tipPercentage are the operands, and the multiplication sign ($*$) is the operator.

Creating Numeric Expressions

In JavaScript, a mathematical calculation is called a *numeric expression*, and it combines numeric operands and arithmetic operators to produce a numeric result. This section discusses all the JavaScript arithmetic operators and shows you how best to use them to build useful and handy numeric expressions.

Table 3-1 lists the basic arithmetic operators you can use in your JavaScript expressions.

JavaScript also comes with a few extra operators that combine some of the arithmetic operators and the assignment operator, which is the humble equals sign (=) that assigns a value to a variable. Table 3-2 lists these so-called *arithmetic assignment* operators.

TABLE 3-1 The JavaScript Arithmetic Operators

Operator	Name	Example	Result
+	Addition	10 + 4	14
++	Increment	10++	11
–	Subtraction	10 – 4	6
–	Negation	–10	–10
––	Decrement	10––	9
*	Multiplication	10 * 4	40
/	Division	10 / 4	2.5
%	Modulus	10 % 4	2

TABLE 3-2 The JavaScript Arithmetic Assignment Operators

Operator	Example	Equivalent
+=	x += y	x = x + y
–=	x –= y	x = x – y
*=	x *= y	x = x * y
/=	x /= y	x = x / y
^=	x ^= y	x = x ^ y
%=	x %= y	x = x % y

Building String Expressions

A string expression is one where at least one of the operands is a string, and the result of the expression is another string. String expressions are straightforward in the sense that there is only one operator to deal with: *concatenation* (+). You use this operator to combine (or *concatenate*) strings within an expression. For example, the expression "Java" + "Script" returns the string "JavaScript". Note, however, that you can also use strings with the comparison operators discussed in the next section.

Building Comparison Expressions

You use comparison expressions to compare the values of two or more numbers, strings, variables, properties, or function results. If the expression is true, the expression result is set to the Boolean value true; if the expression is false, the expression result is set to the Boolean value false. You'll use comparisons with alarming frequency in your JavaScript code, so it's important to understand what they are and how you use them.

Table 3-3 summarizes JavaScript's comparison operators.

TABLE 3-3 The JavaScript Comparison Operators

Operator	Name	Example	Result
==	Equality	10 == 4	false
!=	Inequality	10 != 4	true
>	Greater than	10 > 4	true
<	Less than	10 < 4	false
>=	Greater than or equal	10 >= 4	true
<=	Less than or equal	10 <= 4	false
===	Strict equality	"10" === 10	false
!==	Strict inequality	"10" !== 10	true

Building Logical Expressions

You use logical expressions to combine or manipulate Boolean values, particularly comparison expressions. For example, if your code needs to test whether two different comparison expressions are both true before proceeding, you can do that with a logical expression.

Table 3-4 lists JavaScript's logical operators.

TABLE 3-4 The JavaScript Logical Operators

Operator	Name	General Syntax	Returned Value
&&	AND	*expr1* && *expr2*	true if both *expr1* and *expr2* are true; false otherwise.
||	OR	*expr1* || *expr2*	true if one or both of *expr1* and *expr2* are true; false otherwise.
!	NOT	!*expr*	true if *expr* is false; false if *expr* is true.

Understanding Operator Precedence

In complex expressions, the order in which the calculations are performed becomes crucial. For example, consider the expression 3+5*2. If you calculate from left to right, the answer you get is 16 (3+5 equals 8, and 8*2 equals 16). However, if you perform the multiplication first and then the addition, the result is 13 (5*2 equals 10, and 3+10 equals 13).

To control this ordering problem, JavaScript evaluates an expression according to a predefined *order of precedence*. This order of precedence lets JavaScript calculate an expression unambiguously by determining which part of the expression it calculates first, which part second, and so on.

The order of precedence

The order of precedence that JavaScript uses is determined by the various expression operators that I've covered so far in this chapter. Table 3-5 summarizes the complete order of precedence used by JavaScript.

For example, Table 3-5 tells you that JavaScript performs multiplication before addition. Therefore, the correct answer for the expression 3+5*2 (just discussed) is 13.

TABLE 3-5 The JavaScript Order of Precedence for Operators

Operator	Operation	Order of Precedence	Order of Evaluation
++	Increment	First	R -> L
--	Decrement	First	R -> L
-	Negation	First	R -> L
!	NOT	First	R -> L
*, /, %	Multiplication, division, modulus	Second	L -> R
+, -	Addition, subtraction	Third	L -> R
+	Concatenation	Third	L -> R
<, <=	Less than, less than or equal	Fourth	L -> R
>, >=	Greater than, greater than or equal	Fourth	L -> R
==	Equality	Fifth	L -> R
!=	Inequality	Fifth	L -> R
===	Strict equality	Fifth	L -> R
!==	Strict inequality	Fifth	L -> R
&&	AND	Sixth	L -> R
||	OR	Sixth	L -> R
?:	Ternary	Seventh	R -> L
=	Assignment	Eighth	R -> L
+=, -=, etc.	Arithmetic assignment	Eighth	R -> L

Controlling the order of precedence

Sometimes you want to take control of the situation and override the order of precedence. That may seem like a decidedly odd thing to do, so perhaps an example is in order. Suppose you know the final price of an item and, given the tax rate, you want to know the original (that is, pre-tax) price.

A first pass at the JavaScript calculation may look something like this:

```
retailPrice = totalPrice / 1 + taxRate;
```

This won't work, though. Why not? Well, according to the rules of precedence, JavaScript performs division before addition, so the totalPrice value first is divided by 1 and then is added to the taxRate value, which isn't the correct order.

To get the correct answer, you have to override the order of precedence so that the addition 1 + taxRate is performed first. You override precedence by surrounding that part of the expression with parentheses, as shown in the following code:

```
const retailPrice = totalPrice / (1 + taxRate);
```

In general, you can use parentheses to control the order that JavaScript uses to calculate expressions. Terms inside parentheses are always calculated first; terms outside parentheses are calculated sequentially (according to the order of precedence).

Chapter **4**

Controlling the Flow of JavaScript

With the default script flow, the browser processes the code inside a `script` element or an external JavaScript file one statement at a time. The browser reads and then executes the first statement, reads and then executes the second statement, and so on until it has no more JavaScript left to read and execute.

That statement-by-statement flow seems reasonable, but it's extremely limited. What if you want your code to test some condition and then branch to a specific chunk of code depending on the result of that test? What if you want your code to repeat some statements multiple times, with some change occurring in each repetition? Code that runs tests and code that repeats itself all fall under the rubric of controlling the flow of JavaScript. In this chapter, you explore this fascinating and powerful subject.

Decision-Making with if Statements

A smart script performs tests on its environment and then decides what to do next based on the results of each test. For example, suppose you've declared a variable that you later use as a divisor in an expression. You should test the variable before using it in the expression to make sure that the variable's value isn't 0.

The most basic test is the simple true/false decision (which could also be thought of as a yes/no or an on/off decision). In this case, your program looks at a certain condition, determines whether it's currently true or false, and acts accordingly. Comparison and logical expressions (covered in Chapter 3) play a big part here because they always return a true or false result.

In JavaScript, simple true/false decisions are handled by the if statement. You can use either the *single-line* syntax:

```
if (expression) statement;
```

or the *block* syntax:

```
if (expression) {
    statement1;
    statement2;
    ...
}
```

In both cases, *expression* is a comparison or logical expression that returns true or false, and *statement(s)* represent the JavaScript statement or statements to run if *expression* returns true. If *expression* returns false, JavaScript skips over the statements.

This is a good place to note that JavaScript defines the following values as the equivalent of false: 0, "" (that is, the empty string), null, and undefined. Everything else is the equivalent of true.

This is the first time you've encountered JavaScript's braces ({ and }), so take a second to understand what they do because they come up a lot. The braces surround one or more statements that you want JavaScript to treat as a single entity. This entity is a kind of statement itself, so the whole caboodle — the braces and the code they enclose — is called a *block statement*. Also, any Java-Script construction that consists of a statement (such as if) followed by a block statement is called a *compound statement*. And, just to keep you on your toes, note that the lines that include the braces don't end with semicolons.

Whether you use the single-line or block syntax depends on the statements you want to run if the *expression* returns a true result. If you have only one statement, you can use either syntax. If you have multiple statements, use the block syntax.

Consider the following example:

```
if (totalSales != 0) {
    const grossMargin = (totalSales -
    totalExpenses) / totalSales;
}
```

This code assumes that earlier, the script has calculated the total sales and total expenses, which are stored in the totalSales and totalExpenses variables, respectively. The code now calculates the gross margin, which is defined as gross profit (that is, sales minus expenses) divided by sales. The code uses if to test whether the value of the totalSales variable is not equal to zero. If the totalSales != 0 expression returns true, the gross Margin calculation is executed; otherwise, nothing happens. The if test in this example is righteous because it ensures that the divisor in the calculation — totalSales — is never zero.

Branching with if...else Statements

Using the if statement to make decisions adds a powerful new weapon to your JavaScript arsenal. However, the simple version of if suffers from an important limitation: A false result only bypasses one or more statements; it doesn't execute any of its own. This is fine in many cases, but there will be times when you need to run one group of statements if the condition returns true and a different group if the result is `false`. To handle these scenarios, you need to use an `if...else` statement:

```
if (expression) {
    statements-if-true
} else {
    statements-if-false
}
```

The *expression* is a comparison or logical expression that returns true or false. *statements-if-true* represents the block of statements you want JavaScript to run if *expression* returns true, and *statements-if-false* represents the block of statements you want executed if *expression* returns false.

As an example, consider the following code:

```
let discountRate;
if (currMonth === "December") {
    discountRate = 0.2;
} else {
    discountRate = 0.1;
}
const discountedPrice = regularPrice *
    (1 - discountRate);
```

This code calculates a discounted price of an item, where the discount depends on whether the current month is December. The code assumes that earlier, the script set the value of the current month (`currMonth`) and the item's regular price (`regularPrice`). After declaring the `discountRate` variable, an `if...else` statement checks whether `currMonth` equals December. If it does, `discountRate` is set to 0.2; otherwise, `discountRate` is set to 0.1. Finally, the code uses the `discountRate` value to calculate `discountedPrice`.

TIP

`if...else` statements are much easier to read when you indent the statements within each block, as I've done in my examples. This indentation lets you easily identify which block will run if there is a true result and which block will run if the result is false. I find that an indent of four spaces does the job, but many programmers prefer either two spaces or a tab.

Understanding the Value of Code Looping

There are some who would say that the only real goal of the programmer should be to get the job done. As long as the code produces the correct result or performs the correct tasks in the correct order, everything else is superfluous. Perhaps, but *real* programmers know that the true goal of programming is not only to get the job done, but to get it done *as efficiently as possible*. Efficient scripts run faster, take less time to code, and are usually (not always, but usually) easier to read and troubleshoot.

One of the best ways to introduce efficiency into your coding is to avoid reinventing too many wheels. For example, consider the following code fragment:

```
let sum = 0;
let num = prompt("Type a number:", 1);
sum += Number(num);
num = prompt("Type a number:", 1);
sum += Number(num);
num = prompt("Type a number:", 1);
sum += Number(num);
document.write("The total of your numbers
    is " + sum);
```

This code first declares a variable named sum. The code prompts the user for a number (using the prompt method with a default value of 1) that gets stored in the num variable, adds that value to sum, and then repeats this prompt-and-sum routine two more times. (Note my use of the Number function, which ensures that the value returned by prompt is treated as a number rather than a string.) Finally, the sum of the three numbers is displayed to the user.

Besides being a tad useless, this code just reeks of inefficiency because most of the code consists of the following two lines appearing three times:

```
num = prompt("Type a number:", 1);
sum += Number(num);
```

Wouldn't it be more efficient if you put these two statements just once in the code and then somehow get JavaScript to repeat these statements as many times as necessary?

Why, yes, it would, and the good news is that not only is it possible to do this, but JavaScript also gives you a number of different methods to perform this so-called *looping*. I spend the rest of this chapter investigating each of these methods.

Working with while Loops

The most straightforward of the JavaScript loop constructions is the while loop, which uses the following syntax:

```
while (expression) {
    statements
}
```

Here, *expression* is a comparison or logical expression (that is, an expression that returns true or false) that, as long as it returns true, tells JavaScript to keep executing the *statements* within the block.

Essentially, JavaScript interprets a while loop as follows: "Okay, as long as *expression* remains true, I'll keep running through the loop statements, but as soon as *expression* becomes false, I'm out of there."

Here's a closer look at how a while loop works:

1. Evaluate the *expression* in the while statement.
2. If *expression* is true, continue with Step 3; if *expression* is false, skip to Step 5.
3. Execute each of the statements in the block.
4. Return to Step 1.
5. Exit the loop (that is, execute the next statement that occurs after the while block).

The following code demonstrates how to use while to rewrite the inefficient code shown in the previous section:

```
let sum = 0;
let counter = 1;
let num;
while (counter <= 3) {
    num = prompt("Type a number:", 1);
    sum += Number(num);
    counter += 1;
}
document.write("The total of your numbers
    is " + sum);
```

To control the loop, the code declares a variable named counter and initializes it to 1, which means that the expression counter <= 3 is true, so the code enters the block, does the prompt-and-sum thing, and then increments counter. This is repeated until the third time through the loop, when counter is incremented to 4, at which point the expression counter <= 3 becomes false and the loop is done.

TIP To make your loop code as readable as possible, always use a two- or four-space indent for each statement in the while block. The same applies to the for and do...while loops that I talk about later in this chapter.

The while statement isn't the greatest loop choice when you know exactly how many times you want to run through the loop. For that, use the for statement, described in the next section. The best use of the while statement is when your script has some naturally occurring condition that you can turn into a comparison expression. A good example is when you're prompting the user for input values. You'll often want to keep prompting the user until they click the Cancel button. The easiest way to set that up is to include the prompt inside a while loop, as shown here:

```
let sum = 0;
let num = prompt("Type a number or click
    Cancel:", 1);
```

```
while (num != null) {
    sum += Number(num);
    num = prompt("Type a number or click
    Cancel:", 1);
}
document.write("The total of your numbers
    is " + sum);
```

The first prompt method displays a dialog box like the one shown in Figure 4-1 to get the initial value; then it stores it in the num variable.

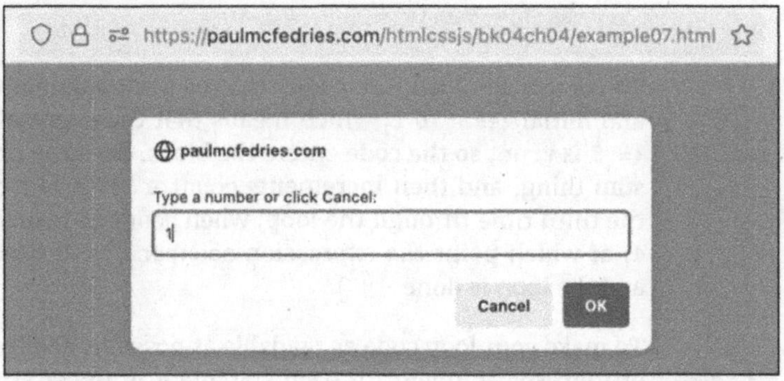

FIGURE 4-1: Set up your while expression so that the prompting stops when the user clicks the Cancel button.

Then the while statement checks the following expression:

```
num != null
```

Two things can happen here:

» If the user enters a number, this expression returns true and the loop continues. In this case, the value of num is added to the sum variable, and the user is prompted for the next number.

» If the user clicks Cancel, the value returned by prompt is null, so the expression becomes false and the looping stops.

Working with for Loops

Although `while` is the most straightforward of the JavaScript loops, the most common type by far is the `for` loop. This fact is slightly surprising when you consider (as you will shortly) that the `for` loop's syntax is a bit more complex than that of the `while` loop. However, the `for` loop excels at one thing: looping when you know exactly how many times you want to repeat a group of statements. This is extremely common in all types of programming, so it's no wonder `for` is so often used in scripts.

The structure of a typical `for` loop looks like this:

```
for (let counter = start; counterExpression;
counterUpdate) {
    statements
}
```

There's a lot going on here, so I'll take it one bit at a time:

» *counter*: A numeric variable used as a *loop counter*. The loop counter is a number that counts how many times the procedure has gone through the loop. (Note that you need to include `let` only if this is the first time you've used the variable in the script.)

» *start*: The initial value of *counter*. This value is usually 1, but you can use whatever value makes sense for your script.

» *counterExpression*: A comparison or logical expression that determines the number of times through the loop. This expression usually compares the current value of *counter* to some maximum value.

» *counterUpdate*: An expression that changes the value of *counter*. This expression is evaluated after each turn through the loop. Most of the time, you'll increment the value of counter with the expression *counter += 1*.

» *statements*: The statements you want JavaScript to execute each time through the loop.

When JavaScript stumbles upon the for statement, it changes into its for-loop outfit and follows this seven-step process:

1. Set *counter* equal to *start*.
2. Evaluate the *counterExpression* in the for statement.
3. If *counterExpression* is true, continue with Step 4; if *counterExpression* is false, skip to Step 7.
4. Execute each of the statements in the block.
5. Use *counterUpdate* to increment (or whatever) *counter*.
6. Return to Step 2.
7. Exit the loop (that is, execute the next statement that occurs after the for block).

As an example, the following code shows how to use for to rewrite the inefficient code shown earlier in this chapter:

```
let sum = 0;
let num;
for (let counter = 1; counter <= 3; counter += 1) {
    num = prompt("Type a number:", 1);
    sum += Number(num);
}
document.write("The total of your numbers
    is " + sum);
```

This is the most efficient version yet because the declaring, initializing, and incrementing of the counter variable all take place within the for statement.

REMEMBER

To keep the number of variables declared in a script to a minimum, always try to use the same name in all your for loop counters. The letters i through n traditionally are used for counters in programming. For greater clarity, you may prefer full words, such as count or counter.

Here's a slightly more complex example:

```
let sum = 0;
for (let counter = 1; counter < 4; counter += 1) {
    let num;
```

```
    let ordinal;
    switch (counter) {
        case 1:
            ordinal = "first";
            break;
        case 2:
            ordinal = "second";
            break;
        case 3:
            ordinal = "third";
    }
    num = prompt("Enter the " + ordinal + "
number:", 1);
    sum += Number(num);
}
document.write("The average is " + sum / 3);
```

The purpose of this script is to ask the user for three numbers and then to display the average of those values. The for statement is set up to loop three times. (Note that counter < 4 is the same as counter <= 3.) The first thing the loop block does is use switch to determine the value of the ordinal variable: If counter is 1, ordinal is set to "first"; if counter is 2, ordinal becomes "second"; and so on. These values enable the script to customize the prompt message with each pass through the loop (check out Figure 4-2). With each loop, the user enters a number, and that value is added to the sum variable. When the loop exits, the average is displayed.

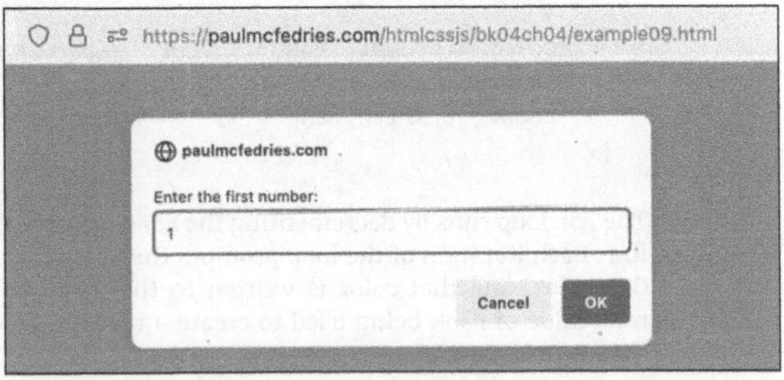

FIGURE 4-2: This script uses the current value of the counter variable to customize the prompt message.

It's also possible to use for to count down. You do this by using the subtraction assignment operator instead of the addition assignment operator:

```
for (let counter = start; counterExpression;
    counter -= 1) {
    statements
}
```

In this case, you must initialize the *counter* variable to the maximum value you want to use for the loop counter, and use the *counterExpression* to compare the value of *counter* to the minimum value you want to use to end the loop.

In the following example, I use a decrementing counter to ask the user to rank, in reverse order, their top three CSS colors:

```
for (let rank = 3; rank >= 1; rank -= 1) {
    let ordinal;
    let color;
    switch (rank) {
        case 1:
            ordinal = "first";
            break;
        case 2:
            ordinal = "second";
            break;
        case 3:
            ordinal = "third";
    }
    color = prompt("What is your " + ordinal +
    "-favorite CSS color?", "");
    document.write(rank + ". " + color + "<br>");
}
```

The for loop runs by decrementing the rank variable from 3 down to 1. Each iteration of the loop prompts the user to type a favorite CSS color, and that color is written to the page, with the current value of rank being used to create a reverse-ordered list, as shown in Figure 4-3.

3. papayawhip
2. lemonchiffon
1. chocolate

FIGURE 4-3: The decrementing value of the rank variable is used to create a reverse-ordered list.

TIP

There's no reason why the for loop counter has to be only incremented or decremented. You're actually free to use any expression to adjust the value of the loop counter. For example, suppose you want the loop counter to run through only the odd numbers 1, 3, 5, 7, and 9. Here's a for statement that will do that:

```
for (let counter = 1; counter <= 9; counter += 2)
```

The expression counter += 2 uses the addition assignment operator to tell JavaScript to increase the counter variable by 2 each time through the loop.

Working with do. . .while Loops

JavaScript has a third and final type of loop that I've left until the last because it isn't one that you'll use all that often. To understand when you might use it, consider this code snippet:

```
let sum = 0;
let num = prompt("Type a number or click
   Cancel:", 1);
while (num != null) {
    sum += Number(num);
    num = prompt("Type a number or click
   Cancel:", 1);
}
```

The code needs the first prompt statement so that the while loop's expression can be evaluated. The user may not feel like entering *any* numbers, and they can avoid it by clicking Cancel in the first prompt box so that the loop will be bypassed.

That seems reasonable enough, but what if your code requires that the user enter at least one value? The following presents one way to change the code to ensure that the loop is executed at least once:

```
let sum = 0;
let num = 0;
while (num !== null || sum === 0) {
    num = prompt("Type a number; when you're
  done, click Cancel:", 1);
    sum += Number(num);
}
document.write("The total of your numbers
  is " + sum);
```

The changes here are that the code initializes both sum and num as 0. Initializing both to 0 ensures that the while expression — num !== null || sum === 0 — returns true the first time through the loop, so the loop will definitely execute at least once. If the user clicks Cancel right away, sum will still be 0, so the while expression — num !== null || sum === 0 — still returns true and the loop repeats once again.

This approach works fine, but you can also turn to JavaScript's third loop type, which specializes in just this kind of situation. It's called a do...while loop, and its general syntax looks like this:

```
do {
    statements
}
while (expression);
```

Here, statements represents a block of statements to execute each time through the loop, and expression is a comparison or logical expression that, as long as it returns true, tells JavaScript to keep executing the statements within the loop.

This structure ensures that JavaScript executes the loop's statement block at least once. How? Take a closer look at how JavaScript processes a do...while loop:

1. Execute each of the statements in the block.

2. Evaluate the *expression* in the while statement.

3. If *expression* is true, return to Step 1; if *expression* is false, continue with Step 4.

4. Exit the loop.

For example, the following shows you how to use do...while to restructure the prompt-and-sum code I showed you earlier:

```
let sum = 0;
let num;
do {
    num = prompt("Type a number; when you're done,
  click Cancel:", 1);
    sum += Number(num);
}
while (num !== null || sum === 0);
document.write("The total of your numbers
  is " + sum);
```

This code is very similar to the while code I show earlier in this section. All that's really changed is that the while statement and its expression have been moved after the statement block so that the loop must be executed once before the expression is evaluated.

Chapter **5**

Harnessing the Power of Functions

Almost every JavaScript project beyond the simplest scripts will require one or more (usually a lot more) tasks or calculations that aren't part of the JavaScript language or any Web API. What's a coder to do? You roll up your sleeves and then roll your own code that accomplishes the task or runs the calculation.

This chapter shows you how to create such do-it-yourself code. In the pages that follow, you explore the powerful and infinitely useful realm of custom functions, where you craft reusable code that performs tasks that out-of-the-box JavaScript can't do.

Getting to Know the Function Structure

A *function* is a group of JavaScript statements that are separate from the rest of the script and that perform a designated task. When your script needs to perform that task, you tell it to run — or *execute*, in the vernacular — the function.

The basic structure of a function looks like this:

```
function functionName([arguments]) {
    JavaScript statements
}
```

Here's a summary of the various parts of a function:

>> `function`: Identifies the block of code that follows it as a function.

>> `functionName`: A unique name for the function. The naming rules and guidelines that I outline for variables in Chapter 2 also apply to function names.

>> `arguments`: One or more values that are passed to the function and that act as variables within the function. Arguments (or *parameters*, as they're sometimes called) are typically one or more values that the function uses as the raw materials for its tasks or calculations. You always enter arguments between parentheses after the function name, and you separate multiple arguments with commas. If you don't use arguments, you must still include the parentheses after the function name.

>> `JavaScript statements`: This is the code that performs the function's tasks or calculations.

Note, too, the use of braces ({ and }). These are used to enclose the function's statements within a block, which tells you (and the browser) where the function's code begins and ends. There are only two rules for where these braces appear:

>> The opening brace must appear after the function's parentheses and before the first function statement.

>> The closing brace must appear after the last function statement.

Making a Function Call

After your function is defined, you'll eventually need to tell the browser to execute — or *call* — the function. There are three main ways to do this:

>> When the browser parses the `<script>` tag

>> After the page is loaded

>> In response to an event, such as the user clicking a button

The next three sections cover each of these scenarios.

When the browser parses the `<script>` tag

The simplest way to call a function is to include in your script a statement consisting of only the function name, followed by parentheses (assuming for the moment that your function uses no arguments). The following code provides an example. (I've listed the entire page to show you where the function and the statement that calls it appear in the page code.)

```
<!DOCTYPE html>
<html lang="en">
<head>
    <meta charset="utf-8">
    <title>Calling a function when the <script>
  tag is parsed</title>
    <script>
        function displayGreeting() {
            const currentHour = new Date().
  getHours();
            if (currentHour < 12) {
                console.log("Good morning!");
            } else {
                console.log("Good day!");
            }
        }
        displayGreeting();
    </script>
</head>
<body>
</body>
</html>
```

The `<script>` tag includes a function named `displayGreeting`, which determines the current hour of the day and then writes a greeting to the console (check out Figure 5-1; you learn about the console in Chapter 9) based on whether it's currently morning. The function is called by the `displayGreeting` statement that appears just after the function.

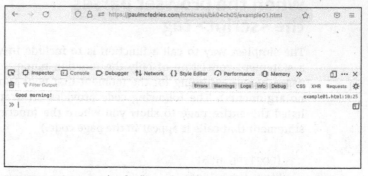

FIGURE 5-1: An example of calling a function when the `<script>` tag is parsed.

When the page load is complete

If your function references a page element, then calling the function from within the page's head section won't work because when the browser parses the script, the rest of the page hasn't loaded yet, so your element reference will fail.

To work around this problem, place another `<script>` tag at the end of the body section, just before the closing `</body>` tag, as shown here:

```
<!DOCTYPE html>
<html lang="en">
<head>
    <meta charset="utf-8">
    <title>Calling a function after the page is
loaded</title>
    <script>
        function makeBackgroundRed() {
            document.body.style.backgroundColor =
"red";
```

```
            console.log("The background is now
red.");
      }
   </script>
</head>
<body>
   <!-- Other body elements go here -->

   <script>
      makeBackgroundRed();
   </script>
</body>
</html>
```

The makeBackgroundRed function does two things: It uses document.body.style.backgroundColor to change the background color of the body element to red, and it uses console.log to write a message to that effect on the console.

In the function, document.body is a reference to the body element, which doesn't "exist" until the page is fully loaded. That means that if you try to call the function with the initial script, you'll get an error. To execute the function properly, a second <script> tag appears at the bottom of the body element, and that script calls the function with the following statement:

```
makeBackgroundRed();
```

By the time the browser executes that statement, the body element exists, so the function runs without an error (check out Figure 5-2).

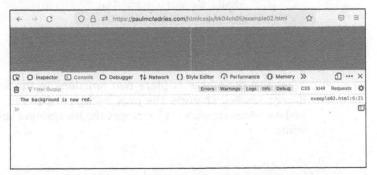

FIGURE 5-2: An example of calling a function after the page has loaded.

When an event fires

One of the most common ways that JavaScript functions are called is in response to some event. Events are such an important topic that I devote a big chunk of Chapter 6 to them. For now, check out a relatively straightforward application: executing the function when the user clicks a button. The following code shows one way to do it:

```
<!DOCTYPE html>
<html lang="en">
<head>
    <meta charset="utf-8">
    <title>Calling a function in response to an
  event</title>
    <script>
        function makeBackgroundRed() {
            document.body.style.backgroundColor=
  "red";
        }
        function makeBackgroundWhite() {
            document.body.style.backgroundColor=
  "white";
        }
    </script>
</head>
<body>
    <button onclick="makeBackgroundRed()">
        Make Background Red
    </button>
    <button onclick="makeBackgroundWhite()">
        Make Background White
    </button>
</body>
</html>
```

What I've done here is place two functions in the script: make BackgroundRed changes the page background to red, as before, and makeBackgroundWhite changes the background color back to white.

The buttons are standard HTML button elements (check out Figure 5-3), each of which includes the onclick attribute. This attribute defines a *handler* — that is, the function to execute — for the event that occurs when the user clicks the button. For example, consider the first button:

```
<button onclick="makeBackgroundRed()">
```

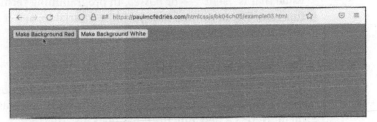

FIGURE 5-3: An example of calling a function in response to an event.

The onclick attribute here says, in effect, "When somebody clicks this button, call the function named makeBackgroundRed."

Passing One or More Values to a Function

One of the main reasons to use functions is to gain control over when some chunk of JavaScript code gets executed. The previous section, for example, discusses how easy it is to use functions to set things up so that code doesn't run until the user clicks a button.

However, there's another major reason to use functions: to avoid repeating code unnecessarily. To understand what I mean, consider the two functions from the previous section:

```
function makeBackgroundRed() {
    document.body.style.backgroundColor= "red";
}
function makeBackgroundWhite() {
    document.body.style.backgroundColor= "white";
}
```

These functions perform the same task — changing the background color — and the only difference between them is that one changes the color to red and the other changes it to white. Whenever you end up with two or more functions that do essentially the same thing, you know that your code is inefficient.

So how do you make the code more efficient? That's where the arguments mentioned earlier come into play. An *argument* is a value that is "sent" — or *passed*, in programming terms — to the function. The argument acts just like a variable, and it automatically stores whatever value is sent.

Passing one value to a function

As an example, you can take the previous two functions, reduce them to a single function, and set up the color value as an argument. Here's a new function that does just that:

```
function changeBackgroundColor(newColor) {
    document.body.style.backgroundColor =
    newColor;
}
```

The argument is named `newColor` and is added between the parentheses that occur after the function name. JavaScript declares `newColor` as a variable automatically, so you don't need a separate `let` or `const` statement. The function then uses the `newColor` value to change the background color. So how do you pass a value to the function? The following code presents a sample file that does so:

```
<!DOCTYPE html>
<html lang="en">
<head>
    <meta charset="utf-8">
    <title>Passing a single value to a function</title>
    <script>
        function changeBackgroundColor(newColor) {
            document.body.style.backgroundColor =
        newColor;
        }
    </script>
```

```
</head>
<body>
    <button onclick="changeBackgroundColor
  ('red')">
        Make Background Red
    </button>
    <button onclick="changeBackgroundColor
  ('white')">
        Make Background White
    </button>
</body>
</html>
```

The key here is the onclick attribute that appears in both
<button> tags. For example:

```
onclick="changeBackgroundColor('red')"
```

The string 'red' is inserted into the parentheses after the function name, so that value is passed to the function itself. The other
button passes the value 'white', and the function result changes
accordingly.

WARNING

In the two onclick attributes in the example code, notice that
the values passed to the function are enclosed in single quotation
marks ('). This is necessary because the onclick value as a whole
is enclosed in double quotation marks (").

Passing two or more values to a function

For more complex functions, you may need to use multiple arguments so that you can pass different kinds of values. If you use
multiple arguments, separate each one with a comma, like this:

```
function changeColors(newBackColor, newForeColor)
  {
    document.body.style.backgroundColor =
  newBackColor;
    document.body.style.color = newForeColor;
  }
```

In this function, the `document.body.style.color` statement changes the foreground color (that is, the color of the page text). The following code shows a revised page where the buttons pass two values to the function:

```
<!DOCTYPE html>
<html lang="en">
<head>
    <meta charset="utf-8">
    <title>Passing multiple values to a function</
    title>
    <script>
        function changeColors(newBackColor,
    newForeColor) {
            document.body.style.backgroundColor =
    newBackColor;
            document.body.style.color =
    newForeColor;
        }
    </script>
</head>
<body>
    <h1>Passing Multiple Values to a Function</h1>
    <button onclick="changeColors('red', 'white')">
        Red Background, White Text
    </button>
    <button onclick="changeColors('white', 'red')">
        White Background, Red Text
    </button>
</body>
</html>
```

WARNING

If you define a function to have multiple arguments, you must always pass values for each of those arguments to the function. If you don't, the "value" `undefined` is passed, instead, which can cause problems.

Getting a Value from a Function

So far, I've outlined two major advantages of using functions:

» You can use them to control when code is executed.

» You can use them to consolidate repetitive code into a single routine.

The third major benefit that functions bring to the JavaScript table is that you can use them to perform calculations and then return the result. As an example, here's a function that calculates the tip on a restaurant bill:

```javascript
function calculateTip(preTip, tipPercent) {
    const tipResult = preTip * tipPercent;
    return tipResult;
}

const preTipTotal = 100.00;
const tipPercentage = 0.15;
const tipCost = calculateTip(preTipTotal,
    tipPercentage);
const totalBill = preTipTotal + tipCost;
document.write("Your total bill is $" +
    totalBill);
```

The function named calculateTip takes two arguments: preTip is the total of the bill before the tip, and tipPercent is the percentage used to calculate the tip. The function then declares a variable named tipResult and uses it to store the calculation — preTip multiplied by tipPercent. The key for this example is the second line of the function:

```javascript
return tipResult;
```

The return statement is JavaScript's way of sending a value *back* to the statement that called the function. That statement comes after the function:

```javascript
tipCost = calculateTip(preTipTotal,
    tipPercentage);
```

This statement first passes the value of preTipTotal (initialized as 100.00 earlier in the script) and tipPercentage (initialized as 0.15 earlier) to the calculateTip function. When that function returns its result, the entire expression calculateTip(preTipTotal, tipPercentage) is replaced by that result, meaning that it gets stored in the tipCost variable. Then preTipTotal and tipCost are added together, the result is stored in totalBill, and a document.write statement displays the final calculation (check out Figure 5-4).

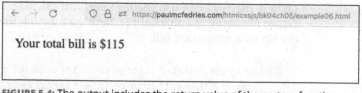

Your total bill is $115

FIGURE 5-4: The output includes the return value of the custom function calculation.

Working with Anonymous Functions

Here's another look at the function syntax from earlier in this chapter:

```
function functionName([arguments]) {
    JavaScript statements
}
```

This version of function syntax creates a so-called *named function* because — you guessed it — the function has a name.

However, creating a function that doesn't have a name is also possible:

```
function ([arguments]) {
    JavaScript statements
}
```

This variety of function syntax creates a so-called *anonymous function* because — that's right — the function has no name.

Why use anonymous functions? Well, first, you don't have to if you don't want to. Second, the main reason to use anonymous functions is to avoid creating a named object when you don't need to. Every large web project has a huge *namespace*, which refers to the full collection of identifiers you assign to things like variables and functions. The larger the namespace, the greater the chance of a *namespace collision*, where you use the same identifier for two different things. Bad news!

Anonymous functions were introduced in ES6, so don't use them if you need to support very old browsers, such as Internet Explorer 11.

If you have a function that will be used only once in your project, it's considered good modern programming practice to make that an anonymous function so that you have one less identifier in your namespace.

Okay, I hear you thinking, earlier you said we invoke a function by using the function name. If an anonymous function has no name, how are we supposed to run it? Excellent question! There are two main methods to look at:

>> Assigning the function to a variable

>> Replacing a function call with the function itself

Assigning an anonymous function to a variable

The example code from the previous section defines the named function calculateTip() and later uses the tipCost variable to store the function result. This is a perfect example of when a named function is not needed because you only ever use the named function to calculate the tipCost value. Adding an identity to the namespace when you don't have to is called *polluting* the namespace, and it's a big no-no in modern JavaScript programming.

You can rewrite this code to use an anonymous function instead:

```
const preTipTotal = 100.00;
const tipPercentage = 0.15;
```

```
// Declare tipCost using an anonymous function
const tipCost = function (preTip, tipPercent) {
    const tipResult = preTip * tipPercent;
    return (tipResult);
}
const totalBill = preTipTotal +
    tipCost(preTipTotal, tipPercentage);
document.write("Your total bill is $" +
    totalBill);
```

The big change here is that now I declare the value of the tipCost variable to be an anonymous function. That anonymous function is the same as the calculateTip() named function from before, just without the name. In the second-last statement, I invoke the anonymous function by using tipCost(preTipTotal, tipPercentage).

Replacing a function call with an anonymous function

One of the most common uses for anonymous functions is when you need to pass a function as an argument to another function. The passed function is known as a *callback* function.

First, here's an example that uses named functions:

```
<body>
    <button id="bgRed">
        Make Background Red
    </button>
    <button id="bgWhite">
        Make Background White
    </button>
    <script>
        function makeBackgroundRed() {
            document.body.style.backgroundColor=
    'red';
        }
        function makeBackgroundWhite() {
            document.body.style.backgroundColor=
    'white';
        }
```

```
            document.getElementById('bgRed').
    addEventListener(
                'click',
            makeBackgroundRed
        );
        document.getElementById('bgWhite').
    addEventListener(
                'click',
                makeBackgroundWhite
        );
    </script>
</body>
```

The script declares two named functions: makeBackgroundRed()
and makeBackgroundWhite(). The code then creates two event
listeners. One of them listens for clicks on the button that has the
id value bgRed and, when a click is detected, runs the makeBack
groundRed() callback function. The other event listener listens
for clicks on the button that has the id value bgWhite and, when a
click is detected, runs the makeBackgroundWhite() callback function. Refer to Chapter 6 to get the details on the document object
and the getElementById() and addEventListener() methods.

Again, you have two functions that don't need to be named, so
you can remove them from the namespace by replacing the call-
backs with anonymous functions. Here's the revised code:

```
<body>
    <button id="bgRed">
        Make Background Red
    </button>
    <button id="bgWhite">
        Make Background White
    </button>
    <script>
        document.getElementById('bgRed').
    addEventListener(
            'click',
            function() {
                document.body.style.
    backgroundColor= 'red';
            }
```

```
        );
        document.getElementById('bgWhite').
    addEventListener(
            'click',
            function() {
                document.body.style.
    backgroundColor= 'white';
            }
        );
    </script>
</body>
```

Working with Arrow Functions

As you progress in JavaScript, you'll find yourself using anonymous functions constantly. When you get to that stage, you'll be
happy to know that ES6 also offers a simpler anonymous function
syntax. That is, instead of using this:

```
function ([arguments]) {
    JavaScript statements
}
```

you can use this:

```
([arguments]) => {
    JavaScript statements
}
```

All I've done here is remove the `function` keyword and replaced it
with the characters = and > between the arguments and the opening brace. The characters => look like an arrow (JavaScripters call
it a *fat arrow*), so this version of the syntax is known as an *arrow
function*.

REMEMBER

Arrow functions are an ES6 invention, so don't use them if you
need to support very old browsers, such as Internet Explorer 11.

For example, here's an anonymous function from a bit earlier (the
"Assigning an anonymous function to a variable" section):

```
// Declare tipCost using an anonymous function
const tipCost = function (preTip, tipPercent) {
    const tipResult = preTip * tipPercent;
    return (tipResult);
}
```

You can rewrite this using an arrow function:

```
// Declare tipCost using an arrow function
const tipCost = (preTip, tipPercent) => {
    const tipResult = preTip * tipPercent;
    return (tipResult);
}
```

If your anonymous function consists of a single statement, you can take advantage of an arrow function feature called *implicit return*:

```
([arguments]) => statement
```

Here, JavaScript assumes that a single-statement function means that the function returns right after executing the statement, so you can leave out the braces and the return keyword. Here's an example:

```
// Declare tipCost using an arrow function with
   implicit return
const tipCost = (preTip, tipPercent) => preTip *
   tipPercent;
```

Similarly, here's one of the anonymous callback functions from the previous section:

```
document.getElementById('bgRed').addEventListener(
    'click',
    function() {
        document.body.style.backgroundColor=
    'red';
    }
);
```

You can rewrite this code as follows to use an arrow function with implicit return:

```
document.getElementById('bgRed').addEventListener(
    'click',
        () => document.body.style.backgroundColor=
    'red'
);
```

Chapter 6

Coding the Document Object Model

I've talked a lot of JavaScript over the past few chapters, but in a very real sense all that has been just the programming equivalent of noshing on a few appetizers. Now it's time to sit down for the main course: programming the Document Object Model.

In this chapter, you explore the fascinating world of the Document Object Model. You learn lots of powerful coding techniques that enable you to make your web pages do almost anything you want them to do. You learn, too, that this is where web coding becomes fun and maybe just a little addictive (in a good way, I promise).

Getting Familiar with Objects

To write truly useful scripts, you have to do what JavaScript was designed to do from the start: Manipulate the web page that it's displaying. That's what JavaScript is all about, and that manipulation can come in many different forms:

» Add text and HTML attributes to an **element**.

» Modify a CSS **property** of a class or other selector.

>> Store some data in the browser's internal **storage**.

>> Validate a **form's** data before submitting it.

The bold items in this list are examples of the "things" that you can work with, and they're special for no other reason than they're programmable. In JavaScript parlance, these "programmable things" are called *objects*.

You can work with objects in JavaScript in any of the following three ways:

>> You can read and make changes to the object's *properties*.

>> You can make the object perform a task by activating a *method* associated with the object.

>> You can define a procedure that runs whenever a particular *event* happens to the object.

Working with object properties

You refer to a property by using the syntax in the following generic expression:

```
object.property
```

>> *object*: The object that has the property

>> *property*: The name of the property you want to work with

For example, consider the following expression:

```
document.location
```

This expression refers to the document object's location property, which holds the address of the document currently displayed in the browser window. (In conversation, you'd pronounce this expression as "document dot location.") The following code shows a simple one-line script that displays this property in the console, as shown in Figure 6-1.

```
console.log(document.location);
```

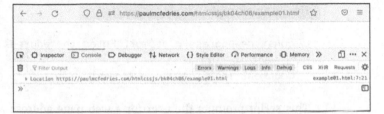

FIGURE 6-1: This script displays the document.location property in a console message.

Because the property always contains a value, you're free to use property expressions in just about any type of JavaScript statement and as an operand in a JavaScript expression. For example, the following statement assigns the current value of the document.location property to a variable named currentUrl:

```
const currentUrl = document.location;
```

Similarly, the following statement includes document.location as part of a string expression:

```
const message = "The current address is " +
    document.location + ".";
```

Some properties are "read only," which means your code can only read the current value and can't change it. However, many properties are "read/write," which means you can also change their values. To change the value of a property, use the following generic syntax:

```
object.property = value
```

Here's what the various parts are:

>> *object*: The object that has the property

>> *property*: The name of the property you want to change

>> *value*: A literal value (such as a string or number) or an expression that returns the value to which you want to set the property

Here's an example:

```
const newAddress = prompt("Enter the address you
    want to surf to:");
document.location = newAddress;
```

This script prompts the user for a web page address and stores the result in the newAddress variable. This value is then used to change the document.location property, which in this case tells the browser to open the specified address.

Working with object methods

To run a method, begin with the simplest case, which is a method that takes no arguments:

```
object.method()
```

Here's what the various parts are:

>> *object*: The object that has the method you want to work with

>> *method*: The name of the method you want to execute

For example, consider the following statement:

```
history.back();
```

This runs the history object's back() method, which tells the browser to go back to the previously visited page.

If a method requires arguments, you use the following generic syntax:

```
object.method (argument1, argument2, ...)
```

For example, consider the confirm() method, used in the following statement, which takes a single argument — a string that specifies the text to display to the user:

```
confirm("Do you want to go back?")
```

Finally, as with properties, if the method returns a value, you can assign that value to a variable (as I do with the confirm( ) method in the earlier example) or you can incorporate the method into an expression.

Introducing the Document Object Model

Here's some source code for a simple web page:

```
<html lang="en">
    <head>
        <title>So Many Kale Recipes</title>
    </head>
    <body>
        <header>
            <h1>Above and Beyond the Kale of
    Duty</h1>
        </header>
        <main>
            <p>
                Do you love to cook with <a
    href="kale.html">kale</a>?
            </p>
        </main>
    </body>
</html>
```

One way to examine this code is hierarchically. That is, the html element is, in a sense, the topmost element because every other element is contained within it. The next level down in the hierarchy contains the head and body elements. The head element contains a title element, which contains the text So Many Kale Recipes. Similarly, the body element contains a header element and a main element.

Hierarchies are almost always more readily grasped in visual form, so Figure 6-2 graphs the page elements hierarchically.

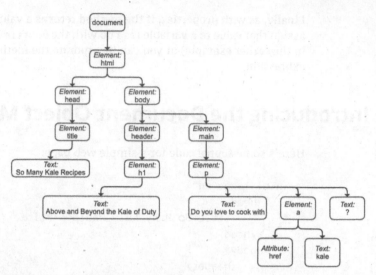

FIGURE 6-2: The web page code as a hierarchy.

REMEMBER

When speaking of object hierarchies, if object P contains object C, object P is said to be the *parent* of object C, and object C is said to be the *child* of object P. In Figure 6-2, the arrows represent parent-to-child relationships. Also, elements on the same level — such as the header and main elements — are known as *siblings*.

You have several key points to consider here:

>> Every box in Figure 6-2 represents an object.

>> Every object in Figure 6-2 is one of three types: element, text, or attribute.

>> Every object in Figure 6-2, regardless of its type, is called a *node*.

>> The page as a whole is represented by the document object.

Therefore, this hierarchical object representation is known as the Document Object Model, or the DOM as it's usually called. The DOM enables your JavaScript code to access the complete structure of an HTML document.

Specifying Elements in Your Code

Elements represent the tags in a document, so you'll be using them constantly in your code. This section shows you several methods for referencing one or more elements.

Specifying an element by id

If it's a specific element you want to work with in your script, you can reference the element directly by first assigning it an identifier using the id attribute:

```
<div id="kale-quotations">
```

With that done, you can then refer to the element in your code by using the document object's getElementById() method:

```
document.getElementById(id)
```

Note: id is a string representing the id attribute of the element you want to work with.

For example, the following statement returns a reference to the previous <div> tag (the one that has id="kale-quotations"):

```
document.getElementById("kale-quotations")
```

WARNING

When you're coding the document object, don't put your <script> tag in the web page's head section (that is, between the <head> and </head> tags). If you place your code there, the web browser will run the code before it has had a chance to create the document object, which means your code will fail, big time. Instead, place your <script> tag at the bottom of the web page, just before the </body> tag.

Specifying elements by tag name

Besides working with individual elements, you can also work with collections of elements. One such collection is the set of all elements in a page that use the same tag name. For example, you could reference all the <a> tags or all the <div> tags.

The mechanism for returning a collection of elements that have the same tag is the getElementsByTagName() method:

```
document.getElementsByTagName(tag)
```

Note: tag is a string representing the HTML name used by the tags you want to work with.

This method returns an array-like collection that contains all the elements in the document that use the specified tag. (Refer to Chapter 7 to find out how arrays work. Also check out "Working with collections of elements," later in this chapter.) For example, to return a collection that includes all the div elements in the current page, you'd use the following statement:

```
const divs = document.getElementsByTagName("div");
```

Specifying elements by class name

Another collection you can work with is the set of all elements in a page that use the same class. The JavaScript tool for returning all the elements that share a specific class name is the getElements ByClassName() method:

```
document.getElementsByClassName(class)
```

Note: class is a string representing the class name used by the elements you want to work with.

This method returns an array-like collection that contains all the elements in the document that use the specified class name. The collection order is the same as the order in which the elements appear in the document. Here's an example:

```
const keywords = document.getElementsByClassName("
    keyword");
```

Specifying elements by selector

The same selectors and combinators that you use with CSS are also available in your JavaScript code to reference page elements by using the document object's querySelector() and query SelectorAll() methods:

```
document.querySelector(selector)
document.querySelectorAll(selector)
```

Note: `selector` is a string representing the selector or combinator for the element or elements you want to work with.

The difference between these methods is that `querySelector All()` returns a collection of all the elements that match your selector, whereas `querySelector()` returns only the first element that matches your selector.

For example, the following statement returns the collection of all section elements that are direct children of an article element:

```
const articles = document.
    querySelectorAll("article > section");
```

Working with collections of elements

The `getElementsByTagName()`, `getElementsByClassName()`, and `querySelectorAll()` methods each return an array-like collection that contains all the elements in the document that use the specified tag, class, or selector, respectively. The collection order is the same as the order in which the elements appear in the document. For example, consider the following HTML code:

```
<div id="div1">
    This, of course, is div 1.
</div>
<div id="div2">
    Yeah, well <em>this</em> is div 2!
</div>
<div id="div3">
    Ignore those dudes. Welcome to div 3!
</div>
```

Now consider the following statement:

```
divs = document.getElementsByTagName("div");
```

In the resulting collection, the first item (`divs[0]`) will be the `<div>` element with id equal to `div1`; the second item (`divs[1]`) will be the `<div>` element with id equal to `div2`; and the third item (`divs[2]`) will be the `<div>` element with id equal to `div3`.

You can also refer to elements directly using their id values. For example, the following statements are equivalent:

```
const firstDiv = divs[0];
const firstDiv = divs.div1;
```

To learn how many items are in a collection, use the length property:

```
const totalDivs = divs.length;
```

To perform one or more operations on each item in the collection, you can use a for...of loop to run through the collection one item at a time. In the JavaScript trade, this is known as *iterating* over the collection. Here's the syntax to use:

```
for (const item of collection) {
    statements
}
```

Here's what the various parts are:

>> *item*: A variable that holds an item in the collection. The first time through the loop, *item* is set to the first element in the collection; the second time through the loop, *item* is set to the second element; and so on.

>> *collection*: The collection of elements you want to iterate over.

>> *statements*: The JavaScript code you want to use to manipulate (or view, or whatever) *item*.

For example, here's some code that iterates over the preceding div elements and displays each item's id value in the console (refer to Chapter 9 for details on the console), as shown in Figure 6-3:

```
divs = document.getElementsByTagName("div");
for (const d of divs) {
    console.log(d.id);
}
```

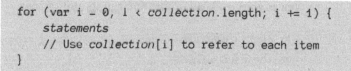

This, of course, is div 1.
Yeah, well *this* is div 2!
Ignore those dudes. Welcome to div 3!

div1		example01.html:19:25
div2		example01.html:19:25
div3		example01.html:19:25

FIGURE 6-3: The output of the script that iterates over the div elements.

WARNING

The for...of loop is an ECMAScript 2015 (ES6) addition. If you need to support ancient browsers such as Internet Explorer 11, you can use a regular for loop, instead:

```
for (var i = 0, i < collection.length; i += 1) {
    statements
    // Use collection[i] to refer to each item
}
```

Touring the DOM with Code

One common task in JavaScript code is working with the children, parent, or siblings of some element in the page. This is known as *traversing the DOM*, because you're using these techniques to move up, down, and along the DOM hierarchy.

In the sections that follow, I use the following HTML code for each example technique:

```
<html lang="en">
    <head>
        <title>So Many Kale Recipes</title>
    </head>
    <body>
        <header id="page-banner">
            <h1>Above and Beyond the Kale of
Duty</h1>
        </header>
```

```
<main id="page-content">
    <p>
        Do you love to cook with <a
href="kale.html">kale</a>?
    </p>
    </main>
  </body>
</html>
```

Getting the children of a parent element

When you're working with a particular element, it's common to want to perform one or more operations on that element's children. Every parent element offers several properties that enable you to work with all or just some of its child nodes:

» All the child nodes

» The first child node

» The last child node

Getting all the child nodes

To return a collection of all the child elements of a parent, you use the children property:

```
parent.children
```

Note: parent is the parent element.

For example, the following statement stores the all the child element nodes of the body element in a variable:

```
const bodyChildElements = document.body.children;
```

The result is an HTMLCollection object, which is an array-like collection of element nodes. If you were to use the console (refer to Chapter 9) to display the value of bodyChildElements, you'd get the output shown in Figure 6-4.

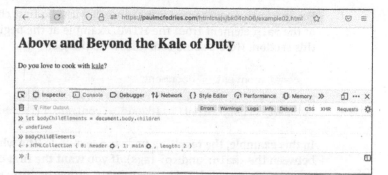

FIGURE 6-4: The value of the bodyChildElements variable displayed in the console.

Here's the output:

```
HTMLCollection { 0: header, 1: main, length: 2 }
```

The numbers 0 and 1 are the index numbers of each child. For example, you could use bodyChildElements[0] to refer to the first element in the collection, which in this example is the header element.

Getting the first child node

If you use a parent element's childNodes or children property to return the parent's child nodes, as I describe in the previous section, you can refer to the first item in the resulting collection by tacking [0] on to the collection's variable name. For example:

```
bodyChildren[0]
bodyChildElements[0]
```

However, the DOM offers a more direct route to the first child node:

```
parent.firstChild
```

Note: parent is the parent element.

For example, suppose you want to work with the first child node of the main element from the HTML example at the beginning of this section. Here's some code that'll do the job:

```
const content = document.
    getElementById("page-content");
const firstContentChildNode = content.firstChild;
```

In this example, the resulting node is a text node (the white space between the `<main>` and `<p>` tags). If you want the first child element node, use the `firstElementChild` property, instead:

```
parent.firstElementChild
```

Note: parent is the parent element.

To get the first child element node of the main element from the code at the beginning of this section, you'd do something like this:

```
const content = document.
    getElementById("page-content");
const firstContentChildElement = content.
    firstElementChild;
```

In this example, this code returns the p element.

Getting the last child node

If your code needs to work with the last child node, use the `lastChild` property of the parent element:

```
parent.lastChild
```

Note: parent is the parent element.

For example, suppose you want to work with the last child node of the p element from the HTML example at the beginning of this section. Here's some code that'll do the job:

```
const para = document.querySelector("main > p");
const lastParaChildNode = para.lastChild;
```

In this example, the resulting node is a text node representing the question mark (?) and the white space to the `</p>` tag. If you want the last child element node, use the `lastElementChild` property, instead:

```
parent.lastElementChild
```

Note: `parent` is the parent element.

To get the last child element node of the p element from the code at the beginning of this section, you could do this:

```
const para = document.querySelector("main > p");
const lastParaChildElement = para.
   lastElementChild;
```

In the example, this code returns the a element.

Getting the parent of a child element

If your code needs to work with the parent of a child element, use the child element's `parentNode` property:

```
child.parentNode
```

Note: `child` is the child element.

For example, suppose you want to work with the parent element of the h1 element from the HTML example at the beginning of this section. Here's some code that'll do the job:

```
const childElement = document.querySelector("h1");
const parentElement = childElement.parentNode;
```

Getting the siblings of an element

A parent's child nodes appear in the DOM in the same order in which they appear in the HTML code, which means the siblings also appear in the order they appear in the HTML. Therefore, for a given child element, there are two sibling possibilities:

>> **Previous sibling:** This is the sibling that appears in the DOM immediately before the child element you're working with. If the child element is the first sibling, it will have no previous sibling.

» **Next sibling:** This is the sibling that appears in the DOM immediately after the child element you're working with. If the child element is the last sibling, it will have no next sibling.

Getting the previous sibling

To return the previous sibling of a particular element, use the previousElementSibling property:

```
element.previousElementSibling
```

Note: element is the element you're working with.

For example, the following statement stores the previous sibling of the main element in a variable:

```
const currElement = document.
    querySelector("main");
const prevSib = currElement.
    previousElementSibling;
```

Getting the next sibling

To return the next sibling of a particular element, use the nextElementSibling property:

```
element.nextElementSibling
```

Note: element is the element you're working with.

For example, the following statement stores the next sibling of the header element in a variable:

```
const currElement = document.
    querySelector("header");
const nextSib = currElement.nextElementSibling;
```

Adding, Modifying, and Removing Elements

After you've got a reference to one or more elements, you can then use code to manipulate those elements in various ways, as shown in the next few sections.

Adding an element to the page

One of the most common web development chores is to add elements to a web page on the fly. When you add an element, you always specify the parent element to which it will be added, and then you decide whether you want the new element added to the end or to the beginning of the parent's collection of children.

To add an element to the page, you follow three steps:

1. Create an object for the type of element you want to add.
2. Add the new object from Step 1 as a child element of an existing element.
3. Insert some text and tags into the new object from Step 1.

Step 1: Creating the element

For Step 1, you use the document object's createElement() method:

```
document.createElement(elementName)
```

Note: elementName is a string containing the HTML element name for the type of the element you want to create.

This method creates the element and then returns it, which means you can store the new element in a variable. Here's an example:

```
const newArticle = createElement("article");
```

Step 2: Adding the new element as a child

With your element created, Step 2 is to add it to an existing parent element. You have four choices:

>> **Append the new element to the end of the parent's collection of child elements:** Use the append( ) method:

```
parent.append(child)
```

Here are the parts of the append( ) method:

- *parent*: A reference to the parent element to which the new element will be appended.
- *child*: A reference to the child element you're appending. Note that you can append multiple elements at the same time by separating each element with a comma. The *child* parameter can also be a text string.

>> **Prepend the new element to the beginning of the parent's collection of child elements:** Use the prepend( ) method:

```
parent.prepend(child)
```

Here are the parts of the prepend( ) method:

- *parent*: A reference to the parent element to which the new element will be prepended.
- *child*: A reference to the child element you're prepending. Note that you can prepend multiple elements at the same time by separating each element with a comma. The *child* parameter can also be a text string.

>> **Insert the new element just after an existing child element of the parent:** Use the after( ) method:

```
child.after(sibling)
```

Here are the parts of the after( ) method:

- *child*: A reference to the child element after which the new element will be inserted.
- *sibling*: A reference to the new element you're inserting. Note that you can insert multiple elements at the same time by separating each element with a comma. The *sibling* parameter can also be a text string.

>> **Insert the new element just before an existing child element of the parent:** Use the before() method:

```
child.before(sibling)
```

Here are the parts of the before() method:

- *child*: A reference to the child element before which the new element will be inserted.

- *sibling*: A reference to the new element you're inserting. Note that you can insert multiple elements at the same time by separating each element with a comma. The *sibling* parameter can also be a text string.

Here's an example that creates a new article element and then appends it to the main element:

```
const newArticle = document.createElement("article");
document.querySelector("main").append(newArticle);
```

Here's an example that creates a new nav element and then prepends it to the main element:

```
const newNav = document.createElement("nav");
document.querySelector("main").prepend(newNav);
```

Step 3: Adding text and tags to the new element

With your element created and appended to a parent, the final step is to add some text and tags using the innerHTML property:

```
element.innerHTML = text
```

Here's what the various parts are:

>> *element*: A reference to the new element within which you want to add the text and tags

>> *text*: A string containing the text and HTML tags you want to insert

WARNING

Whatever value you assign to the `innerHTML` property completely overwrites an element's existing text and tags, so use caution when wielding `innerHTML`. Check out the next section to learn how to insert text and tags rather than overwrite them.

In this example, the code creates a new `nav` element, prepends it to the `main` element, and then adds a heading:

```
const newNav = document.createElement("nav");
document.querySelector("main").prepend(newNav);
newNav.innerHTML = "<h2>Navigation</h2>";
```

Inserting text or HTML into an element

It's often the case that you want to keep the element's existing tags and text and insert new tags and text. Each element offers a couple of methods that enable you do to do this:

>> **To insert just text into an element:** Use the `insertAdjacent Text()` method:

```
element.insertAdjacentText(location, text)
```

Here's what the various parts are:

- *element*: A reference to the element into which the new text will be inserted.
- *location*: A string specifying where you want the text inserted. I outline your choices here shortly.
- *text*: A string containing the text you want to insert.

>> **To insert tags and text into an element:** Use the `insert AdjacentHTML()` method:

```
element.insertAdjacentHTML(location, data)
```

Here's what the various parts are:

- *element*: A reference to the element into which the new tags and text will be inserted.

- *location*: A string specifying where you want the tags and text inserted. I outline your choices here shortly.
- *data*: A string containing the tags and text you want to insert.

For both methods, you can use one of the following strings for the *location* argument:

>> "beforebegin": Inserts the data outside of and just before the element

>> "afterbegin": Inserts the data inside the element, before the element's first child

>> "beforeend": Inserts the data inside the element, after the element's last child

>> "afterend": Inserts the data outside of and just after the element

For example, suppose your document has the following element:

```
<h2 id="nav-heading">Navigation</h2>
```

If you want to change the heading to Main Navigation, the following code will do the job:

```
const navHeading = document.
    getElementById("nav-heading");
navHeading.insertAdjacentText("afterbegin",
    "Main ");
```

Removing an element

If you no longer require an element on your page, you can use the element's remove() method to delete it from the DOM:

```
element.remove()
```

For example, the following statement removes the element with an id value of temp-div from the page:

```
document.getElementById("temp-div").remove();
```

Using Code to Mess Around with CSS

Although you specify your CSS rules in a static stylesheet (.css) file, that doesn't mean that the rules themselves have to be static. With JavaScript on the job, you can modify an element's CSS in a number of ways.

Changing an element's styles

Most elements have a style property that enables you to get and modify a tag's styles. It works like this: The style property actually returns a style object that has properties for every CSS property. When referencing these style properties, you need to keep two things in mind:

» For single-word CSS properties (such as color and visibility), use all-lowercase letters.

» For multiple-word CSS properties, drop the hyphen and use uppercase for the first letter of the second word and for each subsequent word if the property has more than two. For example, the font-size and border-left-width CSS properties become the fontSize and borderLeftWidth style object properties.

Here's an example:

```
const pageTitle = document.querySelector("h1");
pageTitle.style.fontSize = "64px";
pageTitle.style.color = "maroon";
pageTitle.style.textAlign = "center";
pageTitle.style.border = "1px solid black";
```

This code gets a reference to the page's first <h1> element. With that reference in hand, the code then uses the style object to style four properties of the heading: fontSize, color, text-align, and border.

Adding a class to an element

If you have a class rule defined in your CSS, you can apply that rule to an element by adding the class attribute to the element's tag and setting the value of the class attribute equal to the name of your class rule.

First, you can get a list of an element's assigned classes by using the `classList` property:

```
element.classList
```

Note: `element` is the element you're working with.

The returned list of classes is an array-like object that includes an add() method that you can use to add a new class to the element's existing classes:

```
element.classList.add(class)
```

Here's what the various parts are:

>> `element`: The element you're working with.

>> `class`: A string representing the name of the class you want to add to `element`. You can add multiple classes by separating each class name with a comma.

Here's an example, and Figure 6-5 shows the result.

FIGURE 6-5: This code uses the add() method to add the class named my-class to the <div> tag.

CSS:

```
.my-class {
    display: flex;
    justify-content: center;
```

```
    align-items: center;
    border: 6px dotted black;
    font-family: Verdana, serif;
    font-size: 2rem;
    background-color: lightgray;
}
```

HTML:

```
<div id="my-div">
    Hello World!
</div>
```

JavaScript:

```
document.getElementById('my-div').classList.
    add('my-class');
```

REMEMBER

If the class attribute doesn't exist in the element, the addClass() method inserts it into the tag. So in the previous example, after the code executes, the <div> tag now appears like this:

```
<div id="my-div" class="my-class">
```

Removing a class

To remove a class from an element's class attribute, the classList object offers the remove() method:

```
element.classList.remove(class)
```

Here's what the various parts are:

>> element: The element you're working with.

>> class: A string representing the name of the class you want to remove from element. You can remove multiple classes by separating each class name with a comma.

Here's an example:

```
document.getElementById('my-div').classList.
    remove('my-class');
```

Toggling a class

The `classList` object offers the `toggle()` method, which toggles a class on and off an element. That is, it checks the element for the specified class; if the class is there, JavaScript removes it; if the class isn't there, JavaScript adds it. Sweet! Here's the syntax:

```
element.classList.toggle(class)
```

Here's what the various parts are:

>> *element*: The element you're working with

>> *class*: A string representing the name of the class you want to toggle for *element*

Here's an example:

```
document.getElementById('my-div').classList.
   toggle('my-class');
```

Using Code to Tweak HTML Attributes

One of the key features of the DOM is that each tag on the page becomes an element object. You may be wondering, do these element objects have any properties? Yep, they have tons. In particular, if the tag included one or more attributes, those attributes become properties of the element object.

For example, consider the following `<img>` tag:

```
<img id="header-image"
    src="mangosteen.png"
    alt="Drawing of a mangosteen">
```

This tag has three attributes: `id`, `src`, and `alt`. In the DOM's representation of the `<img>` tag, these attributes become properties of the `img` element object. Here's some JavaScript code that references the `img` element:

```
const headerImage = document.
   getElementById("header-image");
```

The `headerImage` variable holds the `img` element object, so your code could now reference the `img` element's attribute values with any of the following property references:

```
headerImage.id
headerImage.src
headerImage.alt
```

However, the DOM doesn't create properties either for custom attributes or for attributes added programmatically. Fortunately, each element object also offers methods that enable you to read any attribute, as well as add, modify, or remove the element's attributes. The next few sections tell all.

Reading an attribute value

If you want to read the current value of an attribute for an element, use the element object's `getAttribute()` method:

```
element.getAttribute(attribute)
```

Here's what the various parts are:

>> *element*: The element you want to work with

>> *attribute*: The name of the attribute you want to read

Here's an example that gets the `src` attribute of the element with an `id` value of `header-image`:

```
const headerImage = document.
   getElementById("header-image");
const srcHeaderImage = headerImage.
   getAttribute("src");
```

Setting an attribute value

To set an attribute value on an element, use the element object's `setAttribute()` method:

```
element.setAttribute(attribute, value);
```

Here's what the various parts are:

>> *element*: The element you want to work with

>> *attribute*: The name of the attribute you want to set

>> *value*: The string value you want to assign to *attribute*

If the attribute already exists, setAttribute overwrites the attribute's current value; if the attribute doesn't exist, setAttribute adds it to the element.

Here's an example that sets the alt attribute for the element with an id value of header-image:

```
const headerImage = document.
   getElementById("header-image");
headerImage.setAttribute("alt", "Lithograph of a
   mangosteen");
```

Removing an attribute

To remove an attribute from an element, use the element object's removeAttribute() method:

```
element.removeAttribute(attribute);
```

Here's what the various parts are:

>> *element*: The element you want to work with

>> *attribute*: A string specifying the name of the attribute you want to remove from the element

Here's an example:

```
const headerImage = document.getElementById
   ("header-image");
headerImage.removeAttribute("id");
```

Listening for Page Events

In web development, an *event* is an action that occurs in response to some external stimulus. A common type of external stimulus is when a user interacts with a web page. Here are some examples:

>> Surfing to or reloading the page
>> Clicking a button
>> Pressing a key
>> Scrolling the page

Why don't web pages respond to events automatically? Why do they just sit there? Because web pages are *static* by default, meaning that they ignore the events that are firing all around them. Your job as a web developer is to change that behavior by making your web pages "listen" for particular events to occur. You do that by setting up special chunks of code called *event handlers*. An event handler consists of two parts:

>> **Event listener:** An instruction to the web browser to watch out ("listen") for a particular event occurring on a particular element.

>> **Callback function:** The code that the web browser executes when it detects that the event has occurred.

You configure your code to listen for and react to an event by setting up an event handler using the element object's addEvent Listener() method. Here's the syntax:

```
element.addEventListener(event, callback);
```

Here's what the various parts are:

>> *element*: The web page element to be monitored for the event. The event is said to be *bound* to the element.

>> *event*: A string specifying the name of the event you want the browser to listen for. For the main events I mention in the previous section, use one of the following, enclosed in quotation marks: DOMContentLoaded, click, dblclick, mouseover, keypress, focus, blur, change, submit, scroll, or resize.

>> *callback*: The callback function that JavaScript executes when the event occurs. The callback can be an anonymous function or a reference to a named function.

Here's an example:

HTML:

```
<div id="my-div"></div>
<button id="my-button">Click to add some text,
  above</button>
```

JavaScript:

```
const myButton = document.
  getElementById('my-button');
myButton.addEventListener('click', function() {
    const myDiv = document.
    getElementById('my-div');
    myDiv.innerHTML = '<h1>Hello Click World!</
  h1>';
});
```

The HTML sets up an empty `div` element and a `button` element. The JavaScript code attaches a `click` event listener to the button, and the callback function adds the HTML string `<h1>Hello Click World!</h1>` to the div. Figure 6-6 shows the resulting page after the button has been clicked.

FIGURE 6-6: The `click` event callback function adds some HTML and text to the `div` element.

If you want to run some code after the web page document has loaded, add an event handler to the document object that listens for the DOMContentLoaded event:

```
document.addEventListener('DOMContentLoaded',
    function() {
        console.log('We are loaded!');
});
```

When an event fires, the DOM creates an Event object, the properties of which contain info about the event, including the following:

>> target: The web page element to which the event occurred. For example, if you set up a click handler for a div element, that div is the target of the click.

>> which: A numeric code that specifies the key that was pressed during a keypress event.

>> pageX: The distance (in pixels) that the mouse pointer was from the left edge of the browser's content area when the event fired.

>> pageY: The distance (in pixels) that the mouse pointer was from the top edge of the browser's content area when the event fired.

>> metaKey: A Boolean value that equals true if the user had the Windows key (🪟) or the Mac Command key (⌘) held down when the event fired.

>> shiftKey: A Boolean value that equals true if the user had the Shift key held down when the event fired.

To access these properties, you insert a name for the Event object as an argument in your event handler's callback function:

```
element.addEventListener(event, function(e) {
    This code runs when the event fires
});
```

Note: e is a name for the Event object that the DOM generates when the event fires. You can use whatever name you want, but most coders use e (although evt and event are also common).

For example, when handling the keypress event, you need access to the which property to find out the code for the key the user pressed. Here's an example page that can help you determine which code value to use:

HTML:

```html
<div>
    Type a key:
</div>
<input id="key-input" type="text">
<div>
    Here's the code of the key you pressed:
</div>
<div id="key-output">
</div>
```

JavaScript:

```javascript
const keyInput = document.
   getElementById('key-input');
keyInput.addEventListener('keypress', function(e)
   {
      const keyOutput = document.
      getElementById('key-output');
      keyOutput.innerHTML = e.which;
});
```

The HTML sets up an `<input>` tag to accept a keystroke, and a `<div>` tag with `id="key-output"` to use for the output. The Java Script code adds a `keypress` event listener to the `input` element, and when the event fires, the callback function writes `e.which` to the output `div`. Figure 6-7 shows the page in action.

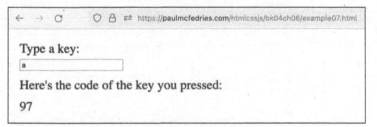

FIGURE 6-7: The `keypress` event callback function uses `e.which` to write the numeric code of the pressed key to the `div` element.

Chapter **7**

Working with Arrays

I n this chapter, you take your coding efficiency to an even higher level by exploring one of JavaScript's most important concepts: the array. Arrays are important not only because they're extremely efficient and very powerful but also because after you know how to use them, you'll think of a thousand and one uses for them. To make sure you're ready for your new array-filled life, this chapter explains what they are and why they're so darn useful, and then explores all the fantastic ways that arrays can make your coding life easier.

What Is an Array?

In JavaScript, whenever you have a collection of variables with related data, you can group them together into a single variable called an *array*. You can enter as many values as you want into the array, and JavaScript tracks each value using an *index number*. For example, the first value you add is given the index 0. The second value you put into the array is given the index 1; the third value gets 2; and so on. You can then access any value in the array by specifying the index number you want.

Declaring an Array

Because an array is a type of variable, you need to declare it before using it. There are four syntaxes you can use. Here's the syntax that's the most informative:

```
const arrayName = new Array();
```

Here, *arrayName* is the name you want to use for the array variable.

In JavaScript, an array is actually an object, so what the new keyword is doing here is creating a new Array object. The Array() part of the statement is called a *constructor* because its job is to construct the object in memory. For example, to create a new array named dogPhotos, you'd use the following statement:

```
const dogPhotos = new Array();
```

The second syntax is useful if you know in advance the number of values (or *elements*) you'll be putting into the array:

```
const arrayName = new Array(num);
```

Here's what the various parts are:

>> *arrayName*: The name you want to use for the array variable

>> *num*: The number of values you'll be placing into the array

For example, here's a statement that declares a new dogPhotos array with five elements:

```
const dogPhotos = new Array(5);
```

Populating an Array

After your array is declared, you can start populating it with the data values you want to store. Here's the general syntax for doing this:

```
arrayName[index] = value;
```

Here's what the various parts are:

>> *arrayName*: The name of the array variable

>> *index*: The array index number where you want the value stored

>> *value*: The value you're storing in the array

JavaScript is willing to put just about any type of data inside an array, including numbers, strings, Boolean values, and even other arrays! You can even mix multiple data types within a single array.

As an example, here are a few statements that declare a new array named dogPhotos and then enter five string values into the array:

```
const dogPhotos = new Array(5);
dogPhotos[0] = "dog-1";
dogPhotos[1] = "dog-2";
dogPhotos[2] = "dog-3";
dogPhotos[3] = "dog-4";
dogPhotos[4] = "dog-5";
```

To reference an array value (say, to use it within an expression), you specify the appropriate index:

```
strURL + dogPhotos[3]
```

Declaring and populating an array at the same time

Earlier, I mentioned that JavaScript has two other syntaxes for declaring an array. Both enable you to declare an array *and* populate it with values by using just a single statement.

The first method uses the Array() constructor in the following general format:

```
const arrayName = new Array(value1, value2, ...);
```

Here's what the various parts are:

>> *arrayName*: The name you want to use for the array variable

>> *value1*, *value2*, ...: The initial values with which you want to populate the array

Here's an example:

```
const dogPhotos = new Array("dog-1", "dog-2",
    "dog-3", "dog-4", "dog-5");
```

JavaScript also supports the creation of *array literals*. You create an array literal by enclosing one or more values in square brackets. Here's the general format:

```
const arrayName = [value1, value2, ...];
```

Here's what the various parts are:

>> *arrayName*: The name you want to use for the array variable

>> *value1*, *value2*, ...: The initial values with which you want to populate the array

An example:

```
const dogPhotos= ["dog-1", "dog-2", "dog-3",
    "dog-4", "dog-5"];
```

Most JavaScript programmers prefer this syntax over using the Array constructor.

Populating an array using a loop

You can populate an array using a loop and some kind of counter variable to access an array's index number programmatically. Here's an example:

```
const dogPhotos = [];
for (let counter = 0; counter < 5; counter += 1) {
    dogPhotos[counter] = "dog-" + (counter + 1);
}
```

The statement inside the `for()` loop uses the variable counter as the array's index. For example, when counter is 0, the statement looks like this:

```
dogPhotos[0] = "dog-" + (0 + 1);
```

In this case, the expression to the right of the equals sign evaluates to `"dog-1"`, which is the correct value.

Iterating Arrays

Arrays can really help make your code more efficient by enabling you to reduce these kinds of long-winded procedures to a much shorter routine that fits inside a function. These routines are iterative methods of the `Array` object, where *iterative* means that the method runs through the items in the array, and for each item, a function (called a *callback*) performs some operation on or with the item.

The `Array` object actually has 14 iterative methods. I don't cover them all, but over the next few sections I talk about the most useful ones.

Iterating an array: forEach()

The `Array` object's `forEach()` method runs a callback function for each element in the array. That callback takes up to three arguments:

» *value*: The value of the element

» *index*: (Optional) The array index of the element

» *array*: (Optional) The array being iterated

You can use any of the following syntaxes:

```
array.forEach(namedFunction);
array.forEach(function (value, index, array) {
    code });
array.forEach((value, index, array ) => { code });
```

Here's what the various parts are:

» *array*: The Array object you want to iterate over.

» *namedFunction*: The name of an existing function. This function should accept the *value* argument and perhaps also the optional *index* and *array* arguments.

» *code*: The statements to run during each iteration.

Here's an example:

```
// Declare the array
const dogPhotos= ["dog-1", "dog-2", "dog-3",
    "dog-4", "dog-5"];

// Iterate through the array
dogPhotos.forEach((value, index) => {
    console.log("Element " + index + " has the
    value " + value);
});
```

Iterating to create a new array: map()

When you iterate over an array, it's common to apply some operation to each element value. In some cases, however, you want to preserve the original array values and create a new array that contains the updated values.

The easiest way to create a new array that stores updated values of an existing array is to use the Array object's map() method. There are three syntaxes you can use:

```
array.map(namedFunction);
array.map(function (value, index, array) { code });
array.map((value, index, array ) => { code });
```

Here's what the various parts are:

» *array*: The Array object with the values you want to use.

» *namedFunction*: The name of an existing function that performs the operation on each array value. This function should accept the *value* argument and perhaps also the optional *index* and *array* arguments.

» *code*: The statements to run during each iteration to perform the operation on each value.

The map() method returns an Array object that contains the updated values, so be sure to store the result in a variable.

Here's an example:

```
// Declare an array of Fahrenheit temperatures
const tempsFahrenheit = [-40, 0, 32, 100, 212];

// Convert each array value to Celsius
const tempsCelsius = tempsFahrenheit.
  map(currentTemp => {
    return (currentTemp - 32) * 0.5556;
});

// Output the result
console.log(tempsCelsius);
```

Iterating an array down to a value: reduce()

One common iteration pattern is to perform a cumulative operation on every element in an array to produce a value. For example, you may want to know the sum of all the values in the array.

Iterating an array in this way to produce a value is the job of the Array object's reduce() method. There are three syntaxes you can use:

```
array.reduce(namedFunction, initialValue);
array.reduce(function (accumulator, value, index,
   array) { code }, initialValue);
array.reduce((accumulator, value, index, array) =>
   { code }, initialValue);
```

Here's what the various parts are:

» *array*: The Array object with the values you want to reduce.

» *namedFunction*: The name of an existing function that performs the reducing operation on each array value. This function should accept the *accumulator* and *value* arguments and perhaps also the optional *index* and *array* arguments.

» *code*: The statements to run during each iteration to perform the reducing operation on each value.

» *initialValue*: The starting value of *accumulator*. If you omit *initialValue*, JavaScript uses the value of the first element in *array*.

Here's an example:

```
// Declare an array of product inventory
const unitsInStock = [547, 213, 156, 844, 449, 71,
    313, 117];

// Get the total units in stock
const initialUnits = 0;
const totalUnits = unitsInStock.reduce
    ((accumulatedUnits, currentInventoryValue) => {
      return accumulatedUnits +
    currentInventoryValue;
}, initialUnits);

// Output the result
console.log("Total units in stock: " + total
    Units);
```

Iterating to locate an element: find()

To search within an array for the first element that matches some condition, use the Array object's find() method. There are three syntaxes you can use:

```
array.find(namedFunction);
array.find(function (value, index, array) { code });
array.find((value, index, array ) => { code });
```

Here's what the various parts are:

>> *array*: The Array object with the values in which you want to search.

>> *namedFunction*: The name of an existing function that applies the condition to each array value. This function should accept the *value* argument and perhaps also the optional *index* and *array* arguments.

>> *code*: The statements to run during each iteration to apply the condition to each value.

In the *namedFunction* or *code*, you set up a logical condition that tests each element in the array and use a return statement to send the result of the test back to the find( ) method. The final value returned by find( ) is the first element for which the test is true, or undefined if the test is false for all the array elements.

Here's an example:

```
// Declare an array of product objects
const products = [
    { name: 'doodad', units: 547 },
    { name: 'gizmo', units: 213 },
    { name: 'gimcrackery', units: 156 },
    { name: 'knickknack', units: 844 },
    { name: 'bric-a-brac', units: 449 },
    { name: 'thingamajig', units: 71 },
    { name: 'watchamacallit', units: 313 },
    { name: 'widget', units: 117 }
];

// Query the array
const strQuery = "gizmo";
```

```
const stock = products.find((currentProduct) => {
    return currentProduct.name === strQuery;
});

// Output the result
if (stock) {
    console.log("Product " + stock.name + " has "
  + stock.units + " units in stock.");
    } else {
    console.log("Product " + strQuery + " not
  found.");
}
```

Manipulating Arrays

Like any good object, Array comes with a large collection of properties and methods that you can work with and manipulate. The
rest of this chapter takes a look at a few of the most useful of
these properties and methods.

The length property

The Array object has just a couple of properties, but the only one
of these that you'll use frequently is the length property:

```
array.length
```

The length property returns the number of elements that are
currently in the specified array.

Some useful array methods

Many methods are associated with arrays, but the proverbial
space limitations prevent me from going into them in any detail.
To whet your appetite, Table 7-1 lists a few of the most useful
array methods.

TABLE 7-1 Useful Array Methods

Method	Syntax	Description
concat()	*array*.concat(*array1*, *array2*, ...)	Takes the elements of one or more existing arrays and concatenates them to an existing array to create a new array.
join()	*array*.join(*separator*)	Takes the existing values in an array and concatenates them to form a string.
pop()	*array*.pop()	Removes the last element from an array and returns the value of that element.
push()	*array*.push(*value1*, *value2*, ...)	Adds one or more elements to the end of an array.
reverse()	*array*.reverse()	Reverses the order of the element in the specified array.
shift()	*array*.shift()	Removes the first element from an array and returns the value of that element.
slice()	*array*.slice(*start*, *end*)	Returns a new array that contains a subset of the elements in an existing array.
sort()	*array*.sort()	Sorts the specified array.
unshift()	*array*.unshift(*value1*, *value2*, ...)	Inserts one or more values at the beginning of an array and returns the new length of the array.

Chapter **8**
Coding Strings and Dates

lthough your JavaScript code will spend much of its time dealing with web page knickknacks such as HTML tags and CSS properties, it will also perform lots of behind-the-scenes chores that require manipulating strings and dealing with dates and times. To help you through these tasks, in this chapter you explore two of JavaScript's built-in objects: the String object and the Date object. You investigate the most important properties of each object and master the most used methods.

Manipulating Strings

I've used dozens of examples of strings so far in this book. These include not only string literals (such as "JavaScript Essentials For Dummies") but also methods that return strings (such as the prompt() method). So, it should be clear by now that strings play a major role in all JavaScript programming, and it will be a rare script that doesn't have to deal with strings in some fashion.

For this reason, it pays to become proficient at manipulating strings, which includes locating text within a string and extracting text from a string. You'll find out about all that and more in this section.

Any string you work with — whether it's a string literal or the result of a method or function that returns a string — is a String object. So, for example, the following two statements are equivalent:

```
const bookName = new String("JavaScript Essentials
    For Dummies");
const bookName = "JavaScript Essentials For
    Dummies";
```

This means that you have quite a bit of flexibility when applying the properties and methods of String objects. For example, the String object has a length property that I describe in the next section. The following are all legal JavaScript expressions that use this property:

```
bookName.length;
"JavaScript Essentials For Dummies".length;
prompt("Enter the book name:").length;
myFunction().length;
```

The last example assumes that myFunction() returns a string value.

Working with string templates

Before diving in to the properties and methods of the String object, take a second to examine a special type of string that's designed to solve three string-related problems that will come up again and again in your coding career:

>> **Handling internal quotation marks:** String literals are surrounded by quotation marks, but what do you do when you need the same type of quotation mark inside the string?

One solution is to use a different type of quotation mark to delimit the string. For example, this is illegal:

```
'There's got to be some better way to do this.'
```

But this is fine:

```
"There's got to be some better way to do this."
```

A second solution is to escape the internal quotation mark with a slash, like so:

```
'There\'s got to be some better way to do this.'
```

These solutions work fine, but *remembering* to use them is harder than you may think!

» **Incorporating variable values:** When you need to use the value of a variable inside a string, you usually end up with something ungainly, such as the following:

```
const adjective = "better";
const lament = "There's got to be some " +
    adjective + " way to do this.";
```

» **Multiline strings:** It's occasionally useful to define a string using multiple lines. However, if you try the following, you'll get a `string literal contains an unescaped line break` error:

```
const myHeader = '
    <nav class="banner">
        <h3 class="nav-heading">Navigation</h3>
        <ul class="nav-links">
            <li>Home</li>
            <li>Away</li>
            <li>In Between</li>
        </ul>
    </nav>'
```

You can solve all three problems by using a *string template* (also called a *template literal*), which is a kind of string literal where the delimiting quotation marks are replaced by back ticks (`` ` ``):

```
`Your string goes here`
```

String templates were introduced as part of ECMAScript 2015 (ES6), so use them only if you don't need to support ancient web browsers such as Internet Explorer 11.

Here's how you can use a string template to solve each of the three problems just described:

» **Handling internal quotation marks:** You're free to plop any number of single or double quotation marks inside a string template:

```
`Ah, here's the better way to do this!`
```

» **Incorporating variable values:** String templates support something called *variable interpolation,* which is a technique for referencing a variable value directly within a string. Here's an example:

```
const adjective = "better";
const paean = `Ah, here's the ${adjective} way
    to do this!`;
```

Within any string template, using ${*variable*} inserts the value of *variable*, no questions asked. Actually, you don't have to stick to just variables. String templates can also interpolate any JavaScript expression, including function results.

» **Multiline strings:** String templates are happy to work error free with strings that are spread over multiple lines:

```
const myHeader = `
    <nav class="banner">
        <h3 class="nav-heading">Navigation</h3>
        <ul class="nav-links">
            <li>Home</li>
            <li>Away</li>
            <li>In Between</li>
    </ul>
</nav>`
```

Determining the length of a string

The most basic property of a String object is its length, which tells you how many characters are in the string:

```
string.length
```

All characters within the string — including spaces and punctuation marks — are counted toward the length. The only exceptions are escape sequences (such as \n), which always count as one character. The following code grabs the length property value for various String object types.

```
function myFunction() {
    return "filename.htm";
}
const bookName = "JavaScript Essentials For
    Dummies";

length1 = myFunction().length; // Returns 12
length2 = bookName.length; // Returns 37
length3 = "123\n5678".length; // Returns 8
```

What the String object lacks in properties, it more than makes up for in methods. There are dozens, and they enable your code to perform many useful tasks, from converting between uppercase and lowercase letters, to finding text within a string, to extracting parts of a string.

Searching for substrings

A *substring* is a portion of an existing string. For example, some substrings of the string "JavaScript" would be "Java", "Script", "vaSc", and "v". When working with strings in your scripts, you'll often have to determine whether a given string contains a given substring. For example, if you're validating a user's email address, you should check that it contains an @ symbol.

Table 8-1 lists the several String object methods that find substrings within a larger string.

TABLE 8-1 String Object Methods for Searching for Substrings

Method	What It Does
string.endsWith(*substring*, *start*)	Tests whether *substring* appears at the end of *string*
string.includes(*substring*, *start*)	Tests whether *substring* appears in *string*
string.indexOf(*substring*, *start*)	Searches *string* for the first instance of *substring*
string.lastIndexOf(*substring*, *start*)	Searches *string* for the last instance of *substring*
string.startsWith(*substring*, *start*)	Tests whether *substring* appears at the beginning of *string*

Learning the methods that extract substrings

Finding a substring is one thing, but you'll often have to extract a substring, as well. For example, if the user enters an email address, you may need to extract just the username (the part to the left of the @ sign) or the domain name (the part to the right of @). For these kinds of operations, JavaScript offers six methods, listed in Table 8-2.

TABLE 8-2 String Object Methods for Extracting Substrings

Method	What It Does
string.charAt(*index*)	Returns the character in *string* that's at the index position specified by *index*
string.charCodeAt(*index*)	Returns the code of the character in *string* that's at the index position specified by *index*
string.slice(*start*, *end*)	Returns the substring in *string* that starts at the index position specified by *start* and ends immediately before the index position specified by *end*

Method	What It Does
string.split(*separator*, *limit*)	Returns an array where each item is a substring in *string*, where those substrings are separated by the *separator* character
string.substr(*start*, *length*)	Returns the substring in *string* that starts at the index position specified by *start* and is *length* characters long
string.substring(start, end)	Returns the substring in *string* that starts at the index position specified by *start* and ends immediately before the index position specified by *end*

Dealing with Dates and Times

Dates and times seem like the kind of things that ought to be straightforward programming propositions. After all, there are only 12 months in a year, 28 to 31 days in a month, seven days in a week, 24 hours in a day, 60 minutes in an hour, and 60 seconds in a minute. Surely something so set in stone couldn't get even the least bit weird, could it?

You'd be surprised. Dates and times *can* get strange, but they get much easier to deal with if you always keep three crucial points in mind:

>> JavaScript time is measured in milliseconds, or thousandths of a second. More specifically, JavaScript measures time by counting the number of milliseconds that elapsed between January 1, 1970 and the date and time in question. So, for example, *you* might come across the date January 1, 2001, and think, "Ah, yes, the start of the new millennium." *JavaScript,* however, comes across that date and thinks "978220800000."

>> In the JavaScript world, time began on January 1, 1970, at midnight Greenwich Mean Time. Dates before that have *negative* values in milliseconds.

>> Because your JavaScript programs run inside a user's browser, dates and times are almost always the user's *local* dates and times. That is, the dates and times your scripts will manipulate will *not* be those of the server on which your page resides. This means that you can never know what time the user is viewing your page.

Learning the arguments used with the Date object

Before getting to the nitty-gritty of the Date object and its associated methods, I'll take a second to run through the various arguments that JavaScript requires for many date-related features. This will save me from repeating these arguments tediously later on. Table 8-3 has the details.

TABLE 8-3 **Arguments Associated with the Date Object**

Argument	What It Represents	Possible Values
date	A variable name	A Date object
yyyy	The year	Four-digit integers
yy	The year	Two-digit integers
month	The month	The full month name from "January" to "December"
mth	The month	Integers from 0 (January) to 11 (December)
dd	The day of the month	Integers from 1 to 31
hh	The hour of the day	Integers from 0 (midnight) to 23 (11:00 PM)
mm	The minute of the hour	Integers from 0 to 59
ss	The second of the minute	Integers from 0 to 59
ms	The milliseconds of the second	Integers from 0 to 999

Getting to know the Date object

Whenever you work with dates and times in JavaScript, you work with an instance of the Date object. More to the point, when you deal with a Date object in JavaScript, you deal with a specific moment in time, down to the millisecond. A Date object can never be a block of time, and it's not a kind of clock that ticks along while your script runs. Instead, the Date object is a temporal snapshot that you use to extract the specifics of the time it was taken: the year, month, date, hour, and so on.

Specifying the current date and time

The most common use of the Date object is to store the current date and time. You do that by invoking the Date() function, which is the constructor function for creating a new Date object. Here's the general format:

```
const dateToday = new Date();
```

Specifying any date and time

If you need to work with a specific date or time, you need to use the Date() function's arguments. There are five versions of the Date() function syntax (refer to the list of arguments near the beginning of this chapter):

```
const date = new Date("month dd, yyyy hh:mm:ss");
const date = new Date("month dd, yyyy");
const date = new Date(yyyy, mth, dd, hh, mm, ss);
const date = new Date(yyyy, mth, dd);
const date = new Date(ms);
```

The following statements give you an example for each syntax:

```
const myDate = new Date("August 23, 2024
    3:02:01");
const myDate = new Date("August 23, 2024");
const myDate = new Date(2024, 8, 23, 3, 2, 1);
const myDate = new Date(2024, 8, 23);
const myDate = new Date(1692763200000);
```

Getting info about a date

When your script just coughs up whatever Date object value you stored in the variable, the results aren't particularly appealing. If you want to display dates in a more attractive format, or if you want to perform arithmetic operations on a date, you need to dig a little deeper into the Date object to extract specific information such as the month, year, hour, and so on. You do that by using the Date object methods listed in Table 8-4.

TABLE 8-4 Date Object Methods That Extract Date Values

Method Syntax	What It Returns
date.getFullYear()	The year as a four-digit number (1999, 2000, and so on)
date.getMonth()	The month of the year; from 0 (January) to 11 (December)
date.getDate()	The date in the month; from 1 to 31
date.getDay()	The day of the week; from 0 (Sunday) to 6 (Saturday)
date.getHours()	The hour of the day; from 0 (midnight) to 23 (11:00 PM)
date.getMinutes()	The minute of the hour; from 0 to 59
date.getSeconds()	The second of the minute; from 0 to 59
date.getMilliseconds()	The milliseconds of the second; from 0 to 999
date.getTime()	The milliseconds since January 1, 1970 GMT

Setting the date

When you perform date arithmetic, you often have to change the value of an existing Date object. For example, an e-commerce script may have to calculate a date that is 90 days from the date that a sale occurs. It's usually easiest to create a Date object and then use an expression or literal value to change the year, month, or some other component of the date. You do that by using the Date object methods listed in Table 8-5.

TABLE 8-5 Date Object Methods That Set Date Values

Method Syntax	What It Sets
date.setFullYear(*yyyy*)	The year as a four-digit number (1999, 2000, and so on)
date.setMonth(*mth*)	The month of the year; from 0 (January) to 11 (December)
date.setDate(*dd*)	The date in the month; from 1 to 31
date.setHours(*hh*)	The hour of the day; from 0 (midnight) to 23 (11:00 PM)
date.setMinutes(*mm*)	The minute of the hour; from 0 to 59
date.setSeconds(*ss*)	The second of the minute; from 0 to 59
date.setMilliseconds(*ms*)	The milliseconds of the second; from 0 to 999
date.setTime(*ms*)	The milliseconds since January 1, 1970 GMT

Chapter **9**
Debugging JavaScript

J avaScript and modern web browsers offer a ton of top-notch debugging tools that can remove some of the burden of program problem solving. In this chapter, you delve into these tools to explore how they can help you find and fix most programming errors. You also investigate a number of tips and techniques that can go a long way in helping you avoid coding errors in the first place.

Laying Out Your Debugging Tools

All the major web browsers come with a sophisticated set of debugging tools that can make your life as a web developer much easier and much saner. Most web developers debug their scripts using Google Chrome, so I focus on that browser in this chapter. But in this section, I give you an overview of the tools that are available in all the major browsers and how to get at them.

Here's how you open the web development tools in Chrome, Firefox, Microsoft Edge, and Safari:

» **Chrome for Windows:** Click Customize and Control Google Chrome (the three vertical dots to the right of the address bar) and then select More Tools ⇨ Developer Tools. Shortcut: Ctrl+Shift+I.

>> **Chrome for Mac:** Select View ⇨ Developer ⇨ Developer Tools. Shortcut: Option+⌘ +I.

>> **Firefox for Windows:** Click Open Application Menu (the three horizontal lines on the far right of the toolbar) and then select More Tools ⇨ Web Developer Tools. Shortcut: Ctrl+Shift+I.

>> **Firefox for Mac:** Select Tools ⇨ Browser Tools ⇨ Web Developer Tools. Shortcut: Option+⌘ +I.

>> **Microsoft Edge:** Click Settings and More (the three vertical dots to the right of the address bar) and then select More Tools ⇨ Developer Tools. Shortcut: Ctrl+Shift+I.

>> **Safari:** Select Develop ⇨ Show Web Inspector. Shortcut: Option+⌘ +I. If you don't have the Develop menu, select Safari ⇨ Settings, click the Advanced tab, and then select the Show Develop Menu in Menu Bar checkbox.

These development tools vary in the features they offer, but each one provides the same set of basic tools, which are the tools you'll use most often. These basic web development tools include the following:

>> **HTML viewer:** This tab (called Inspector in Firefox and Elements in the other browsers) shows the HTML source code used in the web page. When you hover the mouse pointer over a tag, the browser highlights the element in the displayed page and shows its width and height, as shown in Figure 9-1. When you click a tag, the browser shows the CSS styles applied with the tag, as well as the tag's box dimensions (again, refer to Figure 9-1).

>> **Console:** This tab enables you to view error messages, log messages, test expressions, and execute statements. I cover the Console in more detail in the next section.

>> **Debugging tool:** This tab (called Debugger in Firefox and Sources in the other browsers) enables you to pause code execution, step through your code, watch the values of variables and properties, and much more. This is the most important JavaScript debugging tool, so I cover it in detail later in this chapter.

>> **Network:** This tab tells you how long it takes to load each file referenced by your web page. If you find that your page is slow to load, this tab can help you find the bottleneck.

>> **Web storage:** This tab (called Application in Chrome and Edge and Storage in Firefox and Safari) enables you to examine data stored in the browser.

The selected element is highlighted on the page

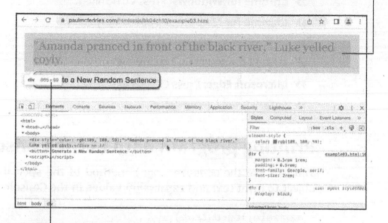

The element's width and height

FIGURE 9-1: The HTML viewer, such as Chrome's Elements tab, enables you to inspect each element's styles and box dimensions.

Debugging 101: Using the Console

If your web page is behaving strangely — for example, the page is blank or missing elements — you should first check your HTML code to make sure it's correct. (Common HTML errors are not finishing a tag with a greater than sign (>), not including a closing tag, and missing a closing quotation mark for an attribute value.) If your HTML checks out, there's a good chance that your JavaScript code is wonky. How do you know? A trip to the Console window is your first step.

The Console is an interactive browser window that shows warnings and errors, displays the output of console.log() statements, and enables you to execute expressions and statements without having to run your entire script. The Console is one of the handiest web browser debugging tools, so you need to know your way around it.

Getting the console onscreen

To display the Console, open your web browser's development tools and then click the Console tab. You can also use the following keyboard shortcuts:

>> **Chrome for Windows:** Press Ctrl+Shift+J.

>> **Chrome for Mac:** Press Option+⌘ +J.

>> **Firefox for Windows:** Press Ctrl+Shift+K.

>> **Firefox for Mac:** Press Option+⌘ +K.

>> **Microsoft Edge:** Press Ctrl+Shift+J.

>> **Safari:** Press Option+⌘ +C.

Printing program data in the Console

You can use the `console.log()` method of the special `Console` object to print text and expression values in the Console:

```
console.log(output)
```

Note: output is the expression you want to print in the Console.

The *output* expression can be a text string, a variable, an object property, a function result, or any combination of these.

TIP

You can also use the handy `console.table()` method to output the values of arrays or objects in an easy-to-read tabular format:

```
console.table(output)
```

Note: output is the array or object (as a variable or as a literal) you want to view in the Console.

For debugging purposes, you most often use the Console to keep an eye on the values of variables, object properties, and expressions. That is, when your code sets or changes the value of something, you insert a `console.log()` (or `console.table()`) statement that outputs the new value. When the script execution is complete, you can open the Console and then check out the logged value or values.

Running code in the Console

One of the great features of the Console is that it's interactive, which means that you can not only read messages generated by the browser or by your `console.log()` statements but also type code directly into the Console. That is, you can use the Console to execute expressions and statements. There are many uses for this feature:

» You can try some experimental expressions or statements to determine their effect on the script.

» When the script is paused, you can output the current value of a variable or property.

» When the script is paused, you can change the value of a variable or property. For example, if you notice that a variable with a value of zero is about to be used as a divisor, you can change that variable to a nonzero value to avoid crashing the script.

» When the script is paused, you can run a function or method to determine whether it operates as expected under the current conditions.

Each browser's Console tab includes a text box (usually marked by a greater-than > prompt) that you can use to enter your expressions or statements.

TIP

You can execute multiple statements in the Console by separating each statement with a semicolon. For example, you can test a for... loop by entering a statement similar to the following:

```
for (let i=1; i < 10; i += 1){console.log(i**2); console.log(i**3);}
```

TIP

If you want to repeat an earlier code execution in the Console, or if you want to run some code that's very similar to code you ran earlier, you can recall statements and expressions that you used in the current browser session. Press the Up Arrow key to scroll back through your previously executed code; press the Down Arrow key to scroll forward through your code.

Putting Your Code into Break Mode

Pausing your code midstream lets you examine certain elements such as the current values of variables and properties. It also lets you execute program code one statement at a time so that you can monitor the flow of the script.

When you pause your code, JavaScript enters *break mode*, which means that the browser displays its debugging tool and highlights the current statement (the one that JavaScript will execute next). Figure 9-2 shows a script in break mode in Chrome's debugger (the Sources tab).

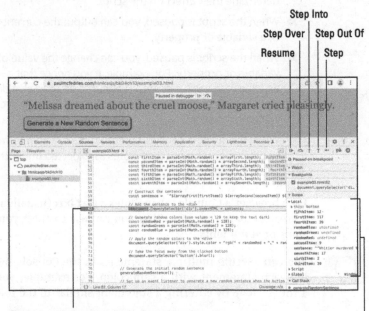

The browser pauses on the current statement

The current values of the script's variables

FIGURE 9-2: When you invoke break mode, the web browser displays its debugging tool and highlights the statement that it will execute next.

Invoking break mode

JavaScript gives you two ways to enter break mode:

» By setting breakpoints

» By using a debugger statement

Setting a breakpoint

If you know approximately where an error or logic flaw is occur-ring, you can enter break mode at a specific statement in the script by setting up a *breakpoint*. Here are the steps to set up a breakpoint:

1. **Display your web browser's developer tools and switch to the debugging tool (such as the Sources tab in Chrome).**

2. **Open the file that contains the JavaScript code you want to debug.**

   How you do this depends on the browser: In Chrome (and most browsers), you have two choices:

   - In the left pane, click the HTML file (if your JavaScript code is within a script element in your HTML file) or the JavaScript (.js) file (if your code resides in an external JavaScript file).

   - Press Ctrl+P (Windows) or ⌘+P (macOS) and then click the file in the list that appears.

3. **Locate the statement where you want to enter break mode.**

   JavaScript will run every line of code up to, but not including, this statement.

4. **Click the line number to the left of the statement to set the breakpoint, as shown in Figure 9-3.**

Deactivate Breakpoints

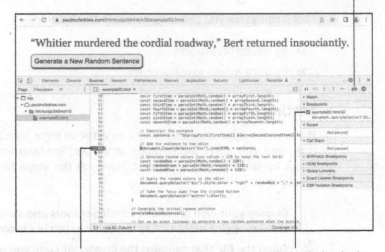

Click a line number to set a breakpoint   Deselect to disable the breakpoint

FIGURE 9-3: In the browser's debugging tool, click a line number to set a breakpoint on that statement.

To remove a breakpoint, most browsers give you three choices:

>> To disable a breakpoint temporarily, deselect the breakpoint's checkbox in the Breakpoints list.

>> To disable all your breakpoints temporarily, click the Deactivate Breakpoint button. Chrome's version of this button is shown here in the margin. Click this button again to reactivate all the breakpoints.

>> To remove a breakpoint completely, click the statement's line number.

Adding a debugger statement

When developing your web pages, you'll often test the robustness of a script by sending it various test values or by trying it out under different conditions. In many cases, you'll want to enter break mode to make sure things appear okay. You could set breakpoints at specific statements, but you lose them if you close the file. For something a little more permanent, you can include a debugger statement in a script. JavaScript automatically enters break mode whenever it encounters a debugger statement.

Here's a bit of code that includes a debugger statement:

```
// Add the sentence to the <div>
document.querySelector('div').innerHTML =
    sentence;
// Generate random colors (use values < 128 to
    keep the text dark)
const randomRed = parseInt(Math.random() * 128);
const randomGreen = parseInt(Math.random() * 128);
const randomBlue = parseInt(Math.random() * 128);
debugger;
```

Getting out of break mode

To exit break mode, you can use either of the following methods in the browser's debugging tool:

>> **Click the Resume button.** Chrome's version of this button is shown here in the margin.

>> **Press the browser's Resume keyboard shortcut.** In Chrome (and most browsers), either press F8 or press Ctrl+\ (Windows) or ⌘ +\ (macOS).

Stepping Through Your Code

One of the most common (and most useful) debugging techniques is to step through the code one statement at a time. Doing so lets you get a feel for the program flow to make sure that things such as loops and function calls are executing properly. You can use four techniques:

>> Stepping one statement at a time

>> Stepping into some code

>> Stepping over some code

>> Stepping out of some code

Stepping one statement at a time

The most common way of stepping through your code is to step one statement at a time. In break mode, stepping one statement at a time means two things:

» You execute the current statement and then pause on the next statement.

» If the current statement to run is a function call, stepping takes you into the function and pauses at the function's first statement. You can then continue to step through the function until you execute the last statement, at which point the browser returns you to the statement after the function call.

To step through your code one statement at a time, set a breakpoint and then, after your code is in break mode, do one of the following to step through a single statement:

» **Click the Step button.** Chrome's version of this button is shown here in the margin.

» **Press the browser's Step keyboard shortcut.** In Chrome (and most browsers, except Firefox, which doesn't support Step as of this writing; use the Step Into button, instead), press F9.

Keep stepping through until the script ends or until you're ready to resume normal execution (by clicking Resume).

Stepping into some code

In all the major browsers (except Firefox), stepping into some code is exactly the same as stepping through the code one statement at a time. The difference comes when a statement executes asynchronously (that is, it performs its operation after some delay rather than right away).

To understand the difference, consider the following code (I've added line numbers to the left; they're not part of the code):

```
1 setTimeout(() => {
2     console.log('Inside the setTimeout()
  block!');
```

```
3 }, 5000);
4 console.log('Outside the setTimeout) block!');
```

This code uses setTimeout() to execute an anonymous function after five seconds. Suppose you enter break mode at the set Timeout() statement (line 1). What happens if you use Step versus Step Into here? Check it out:

>> **Step:** Clicking the Step button doesn't take you to line 2, as you may expect. Instead, because setTimeout() is asynchronous, Step essentially ignores the anonymous function and takes you directly to line 4.

>> **Step Into:** Clicking the Step Into button *does* take you to line 2, but only after the specified delay (five seconds, in this case). You can then step through the anonymous function as needed.

To step into your code, set a breakpoint and then, after your code is in break mode, do one of the following:

>> **Click the Step Into button.** Chrome's version of this button is shown here in the margin.

>> **Press the browser's Step Into keyboard shortcut.** In Chrome (and most browsers), either press F11 or press Ctrl+; (Windows) or ⌘+; (macOS).

REMEMBER

My description of Step Into here doesn't apply (at least as I write this) to Firefox. Instead, the Firefox Step Into feature works like the Step feature I describe in the previous section.

Stepping over some code

Some statements call other functions. If you're not interested in stepping through a called function, you can step over it. Stepping over a function means that JavaScript executes the function normally and then resumes break mode at the next statement *after* the function call.

To step over a function, first either step through your code until you come to the function call you want to step over, or set a breakpoint on the function call and refresh the web page. When you're in break mode, you can step over the function using any of the following techniques:

» **Click the Step Over button.** Chrome's version of this button is shown here in the margin.

» **Press the browser's Step Over keyboard shortcut.** In Chrome (and most browsers), either press F10 or press Ctrl+' (Windows) or ⌘ +' (macOS).

Stepping out of some code

I'm always accidentally stepping into functions I'd rather step over. If the function is short, I just step through it until I'm back in the original code. If the function is long, however, I don't want to waste time stepping through every statement. Instead, I invoke the Step Out feature using any of these methods:

» **Click the Step Out button.** Chrome's version of this button is shown here in the margin.

» **Press the browser's Step Out keyboard shortcut.** In Chrome (and most browsers), either press Shift+F11 or press Ctrl+Shift+; (Windows) or ⌘ +Shift+; (macOS).

JavaScript executes the rest of the function and then reenters break mode at the first line after the function call.

Chapter **10**
Dealing with Form Data

I n this chapter, you learn how to "wire up" your HTML forms by plugging them into some JavaScript code. You explore various form-related objects and then get right to work coding text fields, checkboxes, radio buttons, and selection lists. You also dive into the useful world of form events and even learn how to enhance your form controls with keyboard shortcuts. To top it all off, you go hog wild and learn how to store form data using the Web Storage API.

Coding Text Fields

Text-based fields are the most commonly used form elements, and most of them use the `<input>` tag. The input element has tons of attributes, but from a coding perspective, you're generally interested in only four:

```
<input id="textId" type="textType" name="textName"
    value="textValue">
```

Here's what the various parts are:

» *textId*: A unique identifier for the text field

» *textType*: The kind of text field you want to use in your form

» *textName*: The name you assign to the field

» *textValue*: The initial value of the field, if any

Referencing by field type

One common form-scripting technique is to run an operation on every field of the same type. For example, you may want to apply a style to all the URL fields. Here's the JavaScript selector to use to select all input elements of a given type:

```
document.querySelectorAll('input[type=fieldType]')
```

Note: fieldType is the type attribute value you want to select, such as text or url.

Here's an example where the JavaScript returns the set of all input elements that use the type url:

HTML:

```
<label for="url1">
    Site 1:
</label>
<input id="url1" type="url" name="url1"
    value="https://">
<label for="url2">
    Site 2:
</label>
<input id="url2" type="url" name="url2"
    value="https://">
<label for="url3">
    Site 3:
</label>
<input id="url3" type="url" name="url3"
    value="https://">
```

JavaScript:

```
const urlFields = document.querySelectorAll('input
    [type=url]');
console.log(urlFields);
```

Getting a text field value

Your script can get the current value of any text field by using one of the field object's value-related properties:

```
field.value
field.valueAsDate
field.valueAsNumber
```

Here's an example:

HTML:

```
<label for="search-field">
    Search the site:
</label>
<input id="search-field" name="q" type="search">
```

JavaScript:

```
const searchString = document.
    getElementById('search-field').value;
console.log(searchString);
```

Setting a text field value

To change a text field value, assign the new string to the field object's value property:

```
field.value = value
```

Here's what the various parts are:

>> field: A reference to the form field object you want to work with

>> value: The string you want to assign to the text field

Here's an example:

HTML:

```
<label for="homepage-field">
    Type your homepage address:
</label>
<input id="homepage-field" name="homepage"
  type="url" value="HTTPS://PAULMCFEDRIES.COM/"">
```

JavaScript:

```
const homepageField = document.
  getElementById('homepage-field');
const homepageURL = homepageField.value;
homepageField.value = homepageURL.toLowerCase();
```

The HTML defines an input element of type url where the default value is in all-uppercase letters. The JavaScript code grabs a URL, converts it to all-lowercase characters, and then returns it to the same url field. As shown in Figure 10-1, the text box now displays all-lowercase letters.

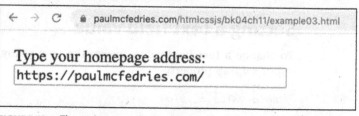

FIGURE 10-1: The script converts the input element's default text to all-lowercase letters.

Programming Checkboxes

You use a checkbox in a web form to toggle a setting on (that is, the checkbox is selected) and off (the checkbox is deselected). You create a checkbox by including in your form the following version of the <input> tag:

```
<input id="checkId" type="checkbox"
  name="checkName" value="checkValue" [checked]>
```

Here's what the various parts are:

>> *checkId*: A unique identifier for the checkbox.

>> *checkName*: The name you want to assign to the checkbox.

>> *checkValue*: The value you want to assign to the checkbox. Note that this is a hidden value that your script can access when the form is submitted; the user never encounters it.

>> checked: When this optional attribute is present, the checkbox is initially selected.

Referencing checkboxes

If your code needs to reference all the checkboxes in a page, use the following selector:

```
document.querySelectorAll('input[type=checkbox]')
```

If you just want the checkboxes from a particular form, use a descendent or child selector on the form's id value:

```
document.querySelectorAll('#formid
    input[type=checkbox]')
```

Or:

```
document.querySelectorAll('#formid >
    input[type=checkbox]')
```

Getting the checkbox state

Your code will want to know whether a checkbox is selected or deselected. This is called the checkbox *state*. In that case, you need to examine the checkbox object's checked property instead:

```
checkbox.checked
```

The checked property returns true if the checkbox is selected, or false if the checkbox is deselected.

Here's an example:

HTML:

```
<label>
    <input id="autosave" type="checkbox"
  name="autosave">
    Autosave this project
</label>
```

JavaScript:

```
const autoSaveCheckBox = document.
  querySelector('#autosave');
if (autoSaveCheckBox.checked) {
    console.log(`${autoSaveCheckBox.name}
  is checked`);
} else {
    console.log(`${autoSaveCheckBox.name}
  is unchecked`);
}
```

The JavaScript code stores a reference to the checkbox object in the `autoSaveCheckBox` variable. Then an `if` statement examines the object's `checked` property and displays a different message in the console, depending on whether `checked` returns `true` or `false`.

Setting the checkbox state

To set a checkbox field to either the selected or deselected state, assign a Boolean expression to the `checked` property:

```
checkbox.checked = true|false
```

For example, suppose you have a form with a large number of checkboxes and you want to set up that form so that the user can select at most three checkboxes. Here's some code that does the job:

```
document.querySelector('form').
    addEventListener('click', event => {

    // Make sure a checkbox was clicked
    if (event.target.type === 'checkbox') {

        // Get the total number of selected
checkboxes
        const totalSelected = document.querySelect
orAll('input[type=checkbox]:checked').length;

            // Are there more than three selected
checkboxes?
            if (totalSelected > 3) {

                // If so, deselect the checkbox that
was just clicked
                event.target.checked = false;
        }
    }
});
```

This event handler runs when anything inside the form element is clicked, and it passes a reference to the click event as the parameter event. Then the code uses the :checked selector to return the set of all checkbox elements that have the checked attribute, and the length property tells you how many are in the set. An if test checks whether more than three are now selected. If that's true, the code deselects the checkbox that was just clicked.

Coding Radio Buttons

You create a radio button using the following variation of the <input> tag:

```
<input id="radioId" type="radio" name="radioGroup"
    value="radioValue" [checked]>
```

Here's what the various parts are:

>> *radioId*: A unique identifier for the radio button.

>> *radioGroup*: The name you want to assign to the group of radio buttons. All the radio buttons that use the same name value belong to that group.

>> *radioValue*: The value you want to assign to the radio button. If this radio button is selected when the form is submitted, this is the value that's included in the submission.

>> checked: When this optional attribute is present, the radio button is initially selected.

Referencing radio buttons

If your code needs to work with all the radio buttons in a page, use this JavaScript selector:

```
document.querySelectorAll('input[type=radio]')
```

If you want the radio buttons from a particular form, use a descendent or child selector on the form's id value:

```
document.querySelectorAll('#formid
    input[type=radio]')
```

Or:

```
document.querySelectorAll('#formid > input
    [type=radio]')
```

If you require just the radio buttons from a particular group, use the following JavaScript selector, where *radioGroup* is the common name of the group:

```
document.querySelectorAll('input[name=
    radioGroup]')
```

Getting a radio button state

If your code needs to know whether a particular radio button is selected or deselected, you need to determine the radio button *state.* You do that by examining the radio button's `checked` attribute, like so:

```
radio.checked
```

The `checked` attribute returns `true` if the radio button is selected, or `false` if the button is deselected.

For example, consider the following HTML:

```
<form>
    <fieldset>
        <legend>
            Select a delivery method
        </legend>
        <label>
            <input type="radio" id="carrier-
pigeon" name="delivery" value="pigeon"
checked>Carrier pigeon
        </label>
        <label>
            <input type="radio" id="pony-express"
name="delivery" value="pony">Pony express
        </label>
        <label>
            <input type="radio" id="snail-mail"
name="delivery" value="postal">Snail mail
        </label>
        <label>
            <input type="radio" id="some-punk"
name="delivery" value="bikecourier">Some punk on
a bike
        </label>
    </fieldset>
</form>
```

If your code needs to know which radio button in a group is selected, you can do that by applying the `:checked` selector to the group and then getting the `value` property of the returned object:

```
const deliveryMethod = document.querySelector('inp
    ut[name=delivery]:checked').value;
```

Setting the radio button state

To set a radio button field to either the selected or deselected state, assign a Boolean expression to the checked attribute:

```
radio.checked = true|false
```

For example, in the HTML code from the previous section, the initial state of the form group had the first radio button selected. You can reset the group by selecting that button. You could get a reference to the id of the first radio button, but what if later you change (or someone else changes) the order of the radio buttons? A safer way is to get a reference to the first radio button in the group, whatever it may be, and then select that element. Here's some code that does this:

```
const firstRadioButton = document.querySelectorAll
    ('input[name=delivery]')[0];
firstRadioButton.checked = true;
```

This code uses querySelectorAll() to return a NodeList collection of all the radio buttons in the delivery group; then it uses [0] to reference just the first element in the collection. Then that element's checked property is set to true.

Programming Selection Lists

Selection lists are common sights in HTML forms because they enable the web developer to display a relatively large number of choices in a compact control that most users know how to operate.

To create the list container, you use the <select> tag:

```
<select id="selectId" name="selectName"
    size="selectSize" [multiple]>
```

Here's what the various parts are:

>> *selectId*: A unique identifier for the selection list.

>> *selectName*: The name you want to assign to the selection list.

- >> *selectSize*: The optional number of rows in the selection list box that are visible. If you omit this value, the browser displays the list as a drop-down box.

- >> multiple: When this optional attribute is present, the user is allowed to select multiple options in the list.

For each item in the list, you add an ‹option› tag between the ‹select› and ‹/select› tags:

```
<option value="optionValue" [selected]>
```

Here's what the various parts are:

- >> *optionValue*: The value you want to assign to the list option.
- >> selected: When this optional attribute is present, the list option is initially selected.

Referencing selection list options

If your code needs to work with all the options in a selection list, use the selection list object's options property:

```
document.querySelector(list).options
```

To work with a particular option within a list, use JavaScript's square brackets operator ([]) to specify the index of the option's position in the list:

```
document.querySelector(list).options[n]
```

Here's what the various parts are:

- >> *list*: A selector that specifies the select element you want to work with
- >> *n*: The index of the option in the returned NodeList collection (where 0 is the first option, 1 is the second option, and so on)

To get the option's text (that is, the text that appears in the list), use the option object's `text` property:

```
document.querySelector(list).options[2].text
```

Getting the selected list option

If your code needs to know whether a particular option in a selection list is selected or deselected, examine the option's `selected` property, like so:

```
option.selected
```

The `selected` attribute returns `true` if the option is selected, or `false` if the option is deselected.

For example, consider the following selection list:

```
<select id="hair-color" name="hair-color">
    <option value="black">Black</option>
    <option value="blonde">Blonde</option>
    <option value="brunette" selected>Brunette
  </option>
    <option value="red">Red</option>
    <option value="neon">Something neon</option>
    <option value="none">None</option>
</select>
```

Your code will likely want to know which option in the selection list is selected. You do that via the list's `selectedOptions` property:

```
const hairColor = document.querySelector('#hair-
    color').selectedOptions[0];
```

This isn't a multi-select list, so specifying `selectedOptions[0]` returns the selected `option` element. In this example, your code could use `hairColor.text` to get the text of the selected option.

If the list includes the `multiple` attribute, the `selectedOptions` property may return an `HTMLCollection` object that contains multiple elements. Your code needs to allow for that possibility by, say, looping through the collection:

HTML:

```
<select id="hair-products" name="hair-products"
    size="5" multiple>
    <option value="gel" selected>Gel</option>
    <option value="grecian-formula"
    selected>Grecian Formula</option>
    <option value="mousse">Mousse</option>
    <option value="peroxide">Peroxide</option>
    <option value="shoe-black">Shoe black</option>
</select>
```

JavaScript:

```
const selectedHairProducts = document.
    querySelector('#hair-products').selectedOptions;
for (const hairProduct of selectedHairProducts) {
    console.log(hairProduct.text);
}
```

Changing the selected option

To set a selection list option to either the selected or deselected state, assign a Boolean expression to the option object's selected property:

```
option.selected = Boolean
```

Here's what the various parts are:

>> *option*: A reference to the option element you want to modify.

>> *Boolean*: The Boolean value or expression you want to assign to the option. Use true to select the option; use false to deselect the option.

Using the HTML code from the previous section, the following statement selects the third option in the list:

```
document.querySelector('#hair-products').
    options[2].selected = true;
```

You can reset the list by deselecting all the options. You do that by setting the selection list object's `selectedIndex` property to –1:

```
document.querySelector('#hair-products').
   selectedIndex = -1
```

Working with Form Events

With all the clicking, typing, tabbing, and dragging that goes on, web forms are veritable event factories. Fortunately, you can let most of these events pass you by, but a few do come in handy, both in running code when the event occurs and in triggering the events yourself.

Most form events are clicks, so you can handle them by setting `click` event handlers using JavaScript's `addEventListener()` method (which I cover in Chapter 6). Here's an example:

HTML:

```
<form>
    <label for="user">Username:</label>
    <input id="user" type="text" name="username">
    <label for="pwd">Password:</label>
    <input id="pwd" type="password"
  name="password">
</form>
```

JavaScript:

```
document.querySelector('form').
   addEventListener('click', () => {
      console.log('Thanks for clicking the form!');
});
```

This example listens for clicks on the entire form element, but you can also create `click` event handlers for buttons, `input` elements, checkboxes, radio buttons, and more.

Setting the focus

One simple feature that can improve the user experience on your form pages is to set the focus on the first form field when your page loads. Setting the focus saves the user from having to make that annoying click inside the first field.

To get this done, run JavaScript's focus() method on the element you want to have the focus at startup:

```
field.focus()
```

Here's an example that sets the focus on the text field with id equal to user at startup:

HTML:

```
<form>
    <label for="user">Username:</label>
    <input id="user" type="text" name="username">
    <label for="pwd">Password:</label>
    <input id="pwd" type="password"
  name="password">
</form>
```

JavaScript:

```
document.querySelector('#user').focus();
```

Monitoring the focus event

Rather than set the focus, you may want to monitor when a particular field gets the focus (for example, by the user clicking or tabbing into the field). You can monitor that by setting up a focus event handler on the field:

```
field.addEventListener('focus', () => {
    Focus code goes here
});
```

Here's an example:

```
document.querySelector('#user').
  addEventListener('focus', () => {
    console.log('The username field has the
  focus!');
});
```

Monitoring the blur event

The opposite of setting the focus on an element is *blurring* an element, which removes the focus from the element. You blur an element by running the blur() method on the element, which causes it to lose focus:

```
field.blur()
```

However, rather than blur an element, you're more likely to want to run some code when a particular element is blurred (for example, by the user clicking or tabbing out of the field). You can monitor for a particular blurred element by setting up a blur() event handler:

```
field.addEventListener('blur', () => {
Blur code goes here
});
```

Here's an example:

```
document.querySelector('#user').
  addEventListener('blur', () => {
    console.log('The username field no longer has
  the focus!');
});
```

Listening for element changes

One of the most useful form events is the change event, which fires when the value or state of a field is modified in some way. When this event fires depends on the element type:

>> For a textarea element and the various text-related input elements, the change event fires when the element loses the focus.

>> For checkboxes, radio buttons, selection lists, and pickers, the change event fires as soon as the user clicks the element to modify the selection or value.

You listen for a field's change events by setting up a change() event handler:

```
field.addEventListener('change', () => {
    Change code goes here
});
```

Here's an example:

HTML:

```
<label for="bgcolor">Select a background color
    </label>
<input id="bgcolor" type="color" name="bg-color"
    value="#ffffff">
```

JavaScript:

```
document.querySelector('#bgcolor').
    addEventListener('change', (event) => {
        const backgroundColor = event.target.value;
        document.body.bgColor = backgroundColor;
});
```

The HTML code sets up a color picker. The JavaScript code applies the change event handler to the color picker. When the change event fires on the picker, the code stores the new color value in the backgroundColor variable by referencing event.target. value, where event.target refers to the element to which the event listener is bound (the color picker, in this case). The code then applies that color to the body element's bgColor property.

Handling Form Data

There's one form event that I didn't cover earlier, and it's a big-gie: the submit event, which fires when the form data is to be sent to the server.

However, if your scripts deal with form data only locally — that is, you never send the data to a server — then you don't need to bother with submitting the form. Instead, it's more straight-forward to add a button to your form and then use that button's click event handler to process the form data in whatever way you need.

Here's an example:

HTML:

```
<form>
    <fieldset>
        <legend>
            Settings
        </legend>
        <label for="background-color">Select a
background color</label>
        <input id="background-color" type="color"
name="bg-color" value="#ffffff">
        <label for="text-color">Select a text
color</label>
        <input id="text-color" type="color"
name="text-color" value="#000000">
        <label for="font-stack">Select a
typeface:</label>
        <select id="font-stack" name="font-stack">
            <option value="Georgia, 'Times New
Roman', serif" selected>Serif</option>
            <option value="Verdana, Tahoma, sans-
serif">Sans-serif</option>
            <option value="'Bradley Hand', Brush
Script MT, cursive">Cursive</option>
            <option value="Luminari">Fantasy</
option>
```

```
                <option value="Monaco, Courier,
    monospace">Monospace</option>
          </select>
          <button>
              Save Your Settings
          </button>
      </fieldset>
</form>
```

JavaScript:

```
// Listen for changes on the #background-color
   color picker
document.querySelector('#background-color').
   addEventListener('change', function() {
const backgroundColor = this.value;
document.body.style.backgroundColor =
   backgroundColor;
});
// Listen for changes on the #text-color color
   picker
document.querySelector('#text-color').
   addEventListener('change', function() {
const textColor = this.value;
document.body.style.color = textColor;
});
// Listen for changes on the #font-stack selection
   list
document.querySelector('#font-stack').
   addEventListener('change', function() {
const fontStack = this.selectedOptions[0].value;
document.body.style.fontFamily = fontStack;
});
// Listen for the button being clicked
document.querySelector('button').
   addEventListener('click', () => {
// Store the form data in a JavaScript object
const userSettings = {
backgroundColor: document.
   querySelector('#background-color').value,
```

```
textColor: document.querySelector('#text-color').
  value,
fontStack: document.querySelector('#font-stack').
  selectedOptions[0].value
}
// Save the settings in local storage
localStorage.setItem('user-settings', JSON.
  stringify(userSettings));
});
```

The HTML sets up a form (check out Figure 10-2) to gather some user settings — background color, text color, and typeface style — as well as a button. The JavaScript sets up change event handlers for the two color pickers and the selection list. Finally, the code listens for click events on the button, and the handler stores the form data in a JavaScript object and then saves the data to local storage.

FIGURE 10-2: A form used to gather user settings for the page.

Chapter **11**

Ten JavaScript Debugging Strategies

G iven any nontrivial JavaScript code, it's a rare (probably nonexistent!) script that runs perfectly the first (or even the tenth!) time. Script bugs happen to even the most experienced developers, so having errors in your code does not mean you're a failure as a coder! All it means is that you're a coder.

But when bugs get into your code, you'll want to exterminate them as quickly as you can. This chapter provides you with ten debugging strategies that can help.

Get Thee to Your Dev Tools

All web page debugging begins with a visit to your web browser development tools. In every browser, the quickest way to open the dev tools is to right-click a page element and then click Inspect. You can also press Ctrl+Shift+I (Windows) or Option⌘+I (macOS).

The Console Is Your Best Debugging Friend

In your code, you can see the current value of a variable or object property by outputting that value to the dev tools Console tab:

```
console.log(output);
```

Replace *output* with the expression you want to print in the Console. The output expression can be a text string, a variable, an object property, a function result, or any combination of these.

Give Your Code a Break(point)

Pausing your code enables you to see what's going on and to run some commands in the console. You have two ways to pause your code mid-execution:

» **Set a breakpoint.** In the dev tools, open the file that contains the JavaScript code, locate the statement where you want to pause, then click the line number to the left of that statement.

» **Add a** debugger **statement.** In your JavaScript code, on the line just before the statement where you want to pause, add a debugger statement.

Step Through Your Code

Once you have some JavaScript code in break mode, use the dev tools execution controls to step through the code. You can step one statement at a time, step over functions, or step into functions.

Monitor Variable and Object Property Values

Either use console.log() statements to output values to the console or, when your code is in break mode, hover the mouse pointer over the variable or object to see its current value in a tooltip. You can also create watch expressions to monitor values.

Indent Your Code

JavaScript code is immeasurably more readable when you indent the code within each statement block. Readable code is that much easier to trace and decipher, so your debugging efforts have one less hurdle to negotiate. Indenting each statement by two or four spaces is typical.

Break Down Complex Tasks

Don't try to solve all your problems at once. If you have a large script or function that isn't working right, test it in small chunks to try to narrow down the problem.

Break Up Long Statements

One of the most complicated aspects of script debugging is making sense out of long statements (especially expressions). The Console window can help (you can use it to print parts of the statement), but it's usually best to keep your statements as short as possible. Once you get things working properly, you can often recombine statements for more efficient code.

Comment Out Problem Statements

If a particular statement is giving you problems, you can temporarily deactivate it by placing two slashes (//) at the beginning of the line. This tells JavaScript to treat the line as a comment. If you have a number of statements you want to skip, place /* at the beginning of the first statement and */ at the end of the last statement.

Use Comments To Document Your Scripts

Speaking of comments, it's a programming truism that you can never add enough explanatory comments to your code. The more comments you add, the easier your scripts will be to debug.

Index

B

back ticks (`` ` ``), 119
backslash (\\), 29
before( ) method, 91
block statements, 40–41
block syntax, 40
blur events, 156
blur( ) method, 156
<body> tag, 6
Boolean
  event values, 102
  expressions
    assigning to object options, 153
    operators, 34
  literals, 30
braces ({ })
  if statements and, 40–41
  as part of function, 56
brackets operator ([ ]), 150
break mode
  debugger statement, 136–137
  entering into, 135–137
  exiting, 137
  overview, 134–137
  Step Into button, 138–139
  Step Out button, 140
  Step Over button, 139–140
  stepping through, 162
breakpoints
  as debugging strategy, 162
  overview, 135–136
browsers
  break mode
    debugger statement, 136–137
    entering into, 135–137
    exiting, 137
    overview, 134–137
    Step Into button, 138–139
    Step Out button, 140
    Step Over button, 139–140
    stepping through code, 162

Console
  accessing, 132
  overview, 130–133
  printing program data in, 132–133
  running code in, 133
  testing code in, 162
ECMAScript 6 and, 12
enabling JavaScript in, 10–12
JavaScript and, 10–13
outdated
  anonymous functions, 67
  arrow functions, 70
  for loop and, 83
  overview, 12–13
parsing <script> tag, 57–58
as requirement to test code, 10
web development tools in
  as debugging strategy, 161
  overview, 129–131

C

callback functions
  overview, 100
  replacing with anonymous functions, 68–71
Cascading Style Sheets (CSS)
  adding classes to element, 94–96
  changing element styles, 94–97
  removing classes, 96
  toggling classes, 97
change( ) event handler, 157
checkboxes
  overview, 144–147
  referencing, 145
children (Document Object Model)
  adding element, 89–91
  getting element, 87
  nodes, 84–87
  overview, 83–84
Chrome, 129–130
classes
  elements and

F

files, external, 14–16
find( ) method, 112–114
Firefox, 130
floating-point numbers, 27
flow of JavaScript, controlling
  loops
    for ... of, 82–83
    do ... while, 51–53
    for, 47–51, 83, 109
    importance of, 43–44
    populating arrays with, 108–109
    structure of, 47
    while, 44–46
  overview, 39
  statements
    if, 40–41
    if.else, 41–42
focus events, 155–156
focus( ) method, 155–156
for ... of loop, 82–83
for loop
  outdated browsers and, 83
  overview, 47–51
  populating arrays with, 109
forEach( ) method, 109–110
form data
  checkboxes
    getting state of, 145–146
    overview, 144–147
    referencing, 145
    setting state of, 146–147
  events
    listening for element changes, 156–157
    monitoring blur, 156
    monitoring focus, 155–156
    overview, 154–157
    setting focus, 155
  handling, 158–160
  radio buttons
    getting state of, 148–149
    overview, 147–150

referencing, 148
setting state of, 150
selection lists
  changing options, 153–154
  getting options, 152–153
  overview, 150–154
  referencing options, 151–152
submitting, 158–160
text fields
  getting values, 143–144
  overview, 141–144
  referencing by type, 142
functions
  anonymous
    assigning to variables, 67–68
    overview, 66–70
    replacing function call with, 68–70
  arguments, 56
  arrow, 70–72
  callback, 68–71, 100
  Date( ), 125
  defined, 8
  document.body, 59
  executing
    browser parsing <script> tag, 57–58
    events, 60–61
    loading web page, 58–59
    overview, 56–57
  find( ), 112–114
  forEach( ), 109–110
  map( ), 110–111
  named, 66
  overview, 55
  reduce( ), 111–112
  structure of, 55–56
  values and
    getting from, 64–66
    passing to, 61–64

G

getAttribute( ) method, 98

methods
  string.slice( ), 122
  string.split( ), 123
  string.substr( ), 123
  string.substring( ), 123
  multiline, 119–120
  null, 28
  object
    determining length of, 121
    manipulating, 117–118
    substrings, 121–123
    templates, 118–120
  prompt( ) method, part of, 23
  substrings
    methods for extracting, 122–123
    searching for, 121–122
styles of element, changing, 94–97
subtraction assignment, 50
syntax
  addEvent.Listener( ) method, 100
  block, 40
  Date( ) function, 125
  declaring arrays, 106
  for ... of loop, 82–83
  objects, 74–77
  single-line, 40

T

tags
  adding to elements, 91–92
  ‹body›, 6
  ‹head›, 6
  ‹img›, 97
  ‹input›
    radio buttons, 147–148
    text fields, 141–145
  ‹noscript›, 11
  ‹script›
    browsers parsing, 57–58
    displaying message to user with, 7–8
    executing functions and, 57–58
    external files and, 15

location of, 79
location within code, 6
overview, 5
writing text to page, 8–10
‹select›, 150
specifying elements by name, 79–80
templates, strings, 118–120
text
  adding to elements, 91–92
  displaying to user, 7–8
  editors, 10
  writing to web pages, 8–10
text fields
  overview, 141–144
  referencing by type, 142
  values and, 142–144
times and dates
  Date object
    arguments for, 124
    methods, 126
    overview, 125–126
    setting dates, 126–127
    specifying, 125
  overview, 123–127
time-sensitive data, displaying on web
  pages, 9
tools in browsers for web development,
  129–131
Torvalds, Linus, 2

U

underscore (_), 24
unshift( ) method, 115
users, displaying messages to
  overview, 7–8
  prompts, 22–23

V

values
  Boleean event, 102
  functions and

About the Author

Paul McFedries is a technical writer who spends his days writing books just like the one you're holding in your hands. In fact, Paul has written more than 100 such books that have sold over four million copies worldwide. Paul invites everyone to drop by his personal website at https://paulmcfedries.com, or to follow him on X (www.twitter.com/paulmcf) or Facebook (www.facebook.com/PaulMcFedries).

Dedication

To Karen, my lobster.

Author's Acknowledgments

Each time I complete a book, the publisher sends me a heavy box filled with a few so-called "author" copies. Opening that box, lifting out a book, feeling the satisfying weight of something that has, up to now, been weightlessly digital, and seeing my name printed on the cover, well, it's a pretty fine feeling, let me tell you. That's pretty cool, but you know what's *really* cool? That I've done that over a hundred times in my writing career, and seeing my name on the cover has *never* gotten old.

But just because mine is the only name you see on the cover, doesn't mean this book was a one-man show. Far from it. Sure, I did write this book's text and take its screenshots, but those represent only a part of what constitutes a "book." The rest of it is brought to you by the dedication and professionalism of Wiley's editing, graphics, and production teams, who toiled long and hard to turn my text and images into an actual book.

I offer my heartfelt thanks to everyone at Wiley who made this book possible, but I'd like to extend some special thank-yous to the folks I worked with directly: Executive Editor Lindsay Berg and Editor Elizabeth Kuball.

Publisher's Acknowledgments

Executive Editor: Lindsay Berg

Editor: Elizabeth Kuball

Production Editor: Saikarthick Kumarasamy

Cover Design and Image: Wiley

Leverage the power

Dummies is the global leader in the reference category and one of the most trusted and highly regarded brands in the world. No longer just focused on books, customers now have access to the dummies content they need in the format they want. Together we'll craft a solution that engages your customers, stands out from the competition, and helps you meet your goals.

Advertising & Sponsorships

Connect with an engaged audience on a powerful multimedia site, and position your message alongside expert how-to content. Dummies.com is a one-stop shop for free, online information and know-how curated by a team of experts.

- Targeted ads
- Video
- Email Marketing
- Microsites
- Sweepstakes sponsorship

20 **MILLION** PAGE VIEWS EVERY SINGLE MONTH

15 MILLION **UNIQUE** VISITORS PER MONTH

43% OF ALL VISITORS ACCESS THE SITE VIA THEIR MOBILE DEVICES

700,000 NEWSLETT SUBSCRIPTIO TO THE INBOXES OF

300,000 UNIQUE INDIVIDUALS EVERY WEEK

# of dummies

Custom Publishing

Reach a global audience in any language by creating a solution that will differentiate you from competitors, amplify your message, and encourage customers to make a buying decision.

- Apps
- Books
- eBooks
- Video
- Audio
- Webinars

Brand Licensing & Content

Leverage the strength of the world's most popular reference brand to reach new audiences and channels of distribution.

For more information, visit dummies.com/biz

PERSONAL ENRICHMENT

Staying Sharp
9781119187790
USA $26.00
CAN $31.99
UK £19.99

Facebook
9781119179030
USA $21.99
CAN $25.99
UK £16.99

Guitar
9781119293354
USA $24.99
CAN $29.99
UK £17.99

Investing
9781119293347
USA $22.99
CAN $27.99
UK £16.99

Beekeeping
9781119310068
USA $22.99
CAN $27.99
UK £16.99

Digital Photography
9781119235606
USA $24.99
CAN $29.99
UK £17.99

Meditation
9781119251163
USA $24.99
CAN $29.99
UK £17.99

Pregnancy
9781119235491
USA $26.99
CAN $31.99
UK £19.99

Samsung Galaxy S7
9781119279952
USA $24.99
CAN $29.99
UK £17.99

iPhone
9781119283133
USA $24.99
CAN $29.99
UK £17.99

Crocheting
9781119287117
USA $24.99
CAN $29.99
UK £16.99

Nutrition
9781119130246
USA $22.99
CAN $27.99
UK £16.99

PROFESSIONAL DEVELOPMENT

Windows 10
9781119311041
USA $24.99
CAN $29.99
UK £17.99

AutoCAD
9781119255796
USA $39.99
CAN $47.99
UK £27.99

Excel 2016
9781119293439
USA $26.99
CAN $31.99
UK £19.99

QuickBooks 2017
9781119281467
USA $26.99
CAN $31.99
UK £19.99

macOS Sierra
9781119280651
USA $29.99
CAN $35.99
UK £21.99

LinkedIn
9781119251132
USA $24.99
CAN $29.99
UK £17.99

Windows 10
9781119310563
USA $34.00
CAN $41.99
UK £24.99

SharePoint 2016
9781119181705
USA $29.99
CAN $35.99
UK £21.99

Fundamental Analysis
9781119263593
USA $26.99
CAN $31.99
UK £19.99

Networking
9781119257769
USA $29.99
CAN $35.99
UK £21.99

Office 2016
9781119293477
USA $26.99
CAN $31.99
UK £19.99

Office 365
9781119265313
USA $24.99
CAN $29.99
UK £17.99

Salesforce.com
9781119239314
USA $29.99
CAN $35.99
UK £21.99

Coding
9781119293323
USA $29.99
CAN $35.99
UK £21.99